EcoLabs & Field Activities

This book was printed with soy-based ink on acid-free recycled content paper, containing 10% POSTCONSUMER WASTE.

HOLT, RINEHART AND WINSTON

A Harcourt Classroom Education Company

Austin • New York • Orlando • Atlanta • San Francisco • Boston • Dallas • Toronto • London

To the Teacher

The lab activities in this booklet fall into two categories: EcoLabs & Field Activities. EcoLabs are indoor activities with an environmental or ecological focus. Field Activities focus on educational outdoor projects, such as wildlife observation, nature surveys, or natural history.

The labs in this booklet are organized into three sections—Life Science, Earth Science, and Physical Science. Each lab includes the following:

- ### TEACHER'S PREPARATORY GUIDE
    This guide provides useful information such as the following:

Purpose	Helpful Hints
Time Required	Cooperative Learning Strategies
Lab Ratings	Teaching Strategies
Advance Preparation	Background Information
Safety Information	Evaluation Strategies

- ### STUDENT WORKSHEETS
    These blackline masters make it easy for students to follow procedures and record data using an effective scientific method. Icons at the top of every worksheet distinguish the labs as one of the following types: Skill Builder, Discovery Lab, Making Models, or Design Your Own Experiment. At the end of most labs, Critical Thinking questions help students process the information they learned and Going Further activities extend student interest and application.

ANSWER KEY

For your convenience, an Answer Key is available in the back of this booklet. The key includes reduced versions of all applicable worksheets, with answers included on each page.

ASSESSMENT

Several labs include a checklist or evaluation form for assessment. The *Assessment Checklists & Rubrics* booklet and the *Classroom Management CD-ROM* also include assessment checklists and rubrics. The most appropriate of those grading tools are recommended in the Evaluation Strategies of each Teacher's Preparatory Guide. Look for the icons at right to identify those tools.

CLASSROOM TESTED & APPROVED

You will also notice this icon, which acknowledges the many teachers around the country who helped ensure the safety, accuracy, and enjoyment of these labs for students.

Credits: page 100

Printed in the United States of America

ISBN 0-03-054418-1
1 2 3 4 5 6   085   03 02 01 00 99

▪ CONTENTS ▪

CONTENTS, CONTINUED

EcoLabs & Field Activities Guidelines for Teachers

Studying environmental topics in the laboratory and venturing into the field is exciting and productive. In order to ensure safe learning experiences for you and your students, please keep the following precautions in mind:

- Be sure students are aware of proper lab-safety procedures. The safety information on pages vi–viii should be handed out to students. Page viii is a short safety contract that students should read, sign, and return to you to verify that they understand proper safety procedures. Additional safety information is available on the *Classroom Management CD-ROM*.

- The following is a list of additional information to keep in mind while conducting field activities:

Know your mission.   Tell students the goal of the field activity in advance. Be sure they have the necessary supplies, permission slips, and other materials they need to participate.

Know the hazards.   Determine whether there are likely to be poisonous plants or dangerous animals where you will be going. Make sure students know how to identify any such species. Also find out about other hazards, such as steep or slippery terrain.

Suit up!   Tell students in advance what kind of clothing is appropriate. Encourage students to dress in a manner that will keep them warm, comfortable, and dry. Encourage students to wear sunglasses, a hat, gloves, rain gear, or other protective gear suitable for local conditions.

Don't feed the bears.   Students should avoid all animals, especially those that may sting, bite, scratch, or otherwise cause injury.

Don't pick that!   Tell students not to pick, touch, or taste any wild plant without first obtaining your permission. Many wild plants can be irritating to the skin or toxic.

Stick together.   Encourage students to travel with a partner at all times and to stay within calling distance of the group.

Report accidents immediately.   Even if an incident seems unimportant, tell students to let you know immediately. Keep a well-stocked first-aid kit handy when working in the field.

Take only pictures, leave only footprints.   Students should not remove anything from a field site without your permission. Direct students to stay on trails when possible to avoid trampling delicate vegetation. Students should take any garbage they produce with them and leave natural areas as they were found.

Safety Guidelines and Symbols for Students

Performing scientific investigations and field activities is exciting and fun, but it can be dangerous if the proper precautions aren't followed. To make sure that your laboratory or field experience is both exciting and safe, follow the general guidelines listed below. Also follow your teacher's instructions, and don't take shortcuts! When you have read and understood all of the information in this section, including the Student Safety Contract, sign your name in the designated space on the contract, and return the contract to your teacher.

GENERAL

Always get your teacher's permission before attempting any lab investigation or field activity. Before beginning, read the procedures carefully, paying attention to safety information and cautionary statements. If you are unsure about what a safety symbol means, look it up on page vii or ask your teacher. If an accident occurs, inform your teacher immediately.

IN THE FIELD

Know your mission.   Know the goal of the field activity in advance. Be sure you have the necessary supplies, permission slips, and other materials you need to participate.

Know the hazards.   Determine whether there are likely to be poisonous plants or dangerous animals where you will be going. Make sure you know how to identify any such species. Also find out about other hazards, such as steep or slippery terrain.

Suit up!   Find out what kind of clothing is appropriate. Dress in a manner that will keep you warm, comfortable, and dry. Wear sunglasses, a hat, gloves, rain gear, or other protective gear suitable for local conditions.

Don't feed the bears.   Avoid all animals, especially those that may sting, bite, scratch, or otherwise cause injury.

Don't pick that!   Don't pick, touch, or taste any wild plant without first obtaining permission from your teacher. Many wild plants can be irritating to your skin or toxic.

Stick together.   Travel with a partner at all times, and stay within visual and calling distance of the group.

Report accidents immediately.   Even if an incident seems unimportant, tell your teacher immediately.

Take only pictures, leave only footprints.   Do not remove anything from a field site without your teacher's permission. Stay on trails when possible to avoid trampling delicate vegetation. Take any garbage you produce with you, and leave natural areas as they were found.

IN THE LAB

General Know the location of all safety equipment, such as fire alarms, fire blankets, and eyewash stations, and the procedures for using them. Know your school's fire-evacuation routes. Don't work alone in the laboratory. Walk with care in the lab, and keep your work area free from unnecessary clutter. Dress appropriately on lab days. If your hair is long, tie it back. Certain products, such as hair spray, are flammable and should not be worn while working near an open flame. Remove dangling jewelry. Don't wear open-toed shoes or sandals in the laboratory.

 Eye Safety Wear approved safety goggles when working around chemicals, any mechanical device, or any type of flame or heating device. If any substance gets in your eyes, notify your teacher.

 Hand Safety Avoid chemical or heat injuries to your hands by wearing protective gloves or oven mitts. Check the materials list in the lab for the type of hand protection you should wear while performing the experiment.

 Clothing protection Wear an apron to protect your clothing from staining, burning, or corrosion.

 Sharp/Pointed Objects Use knives and other sharp instruments with extreme care. Do not cut an object while holding it in your hands. Instead, place it on a suitable work surface for cutting.

 Heat Wear safety goggles when using a heating device or a flame. Wear oven mitts to avoid burns.

 Electricity Avoid using equipment with damaged cords. Be careful around equipment and cords to avoid accidents. Ensure that your hands are dry and that electrical equipment is turned off before you plug it into an outlet.

 Chemicals Wear safety goggles when handling chemicals. Read chemical labels. Wear an apron and latex gloves when working with acids or bases or when told to do so. If a chemical spills on your skin or clothing, notify your teacher and immediately rinse it off with water for at least 5 minutes. Never touch, taste, or smell a chemical or mix any chemicals unless your teacher instructs you to do so.

  Animal and Plant Safety Handle animals only as directed by your teacher. Always treat animals carefully and with respect. Wash your hands thoroughly after handling an animal or any part of a plant.

Glassware Examine all glassware for chips and cracks before using it. Report damaged glassware to your teacher. Glass containers used for heating should be made of heat-resistant glass.

Cleanup Before leaving the laboratory, clean your work area. Wash glass containers with soap and water. Put away all equipment and supplies. Dispose of all chemicals and other materials as directed by your teacher. Make sure all equipment is turned off and unplugged. Wash your hands with soap and water. Never take anything from the laboratory without permission from your teacher.

Safety Contract

Carefully read the Student Safety Contract below. Then write your name in the blank, and sign and date the contract.

STUDENT SAFETY CONTRACT

I will

- [ ] read the lab investigation before coming to class.
- [ ] wear protective equipment as directed to protect my eyes, face, hands, and body while conducting activities.
- [ ] follow all instructions given by the teacher.
- [ ] conduct myself in a responsible manner at all times in a laboratory situation.

I, _____,

have read and agree to abide by the safety regulations as set forth above, as well as any additional printed instructions provided by my teacher or the school district.

I agree to follow all other written and oral instructions given in class.

Signature: _____

Date: _____

SAFETY APPROVED CONTRACT

The Scientific Method

The steps that scientists use to answer questions and solve problems are often called the scientific method. The scientific method is not a rigid procedure. Scientists may use all of the steps or just some of the steps. They may even repeat some steps. The goal of a scientific method is to come up with reliable answers and solutions.

Six Steps of a Scientific Method

1. Ask a Question Good questions come from careful **observations.** You make observations by using your senses to gather information. Sometimes you may use instruments, such as microscopes and telescopes, to extend the range of your senses. As you observe the natural world, you will discover that you have many more questions than answers. These questions drive the scientific method.

Questions beginning with *what, why, how,* and *when* are very important in focusing an investigation, and they often lead to a hypothesis. (You will learn what a hypothesis is in the next step.) Here is an example of a question that could lead to further investigation.

Question: How does acid rain affect plant growth?

2. Form a Hypothesis After you come up with a question, you need to turn the question into a hypothesis. A **hypothesis** is a clear statement of what you expect the answer to your question to be. Your hypothesis will represent your best "educated guess" based on your observations and what you already know. A good hypothesis is one that is testable. If observations and information cannot be gathered or if an experiment cannot be designed to test your hypothesis, it is untestable, and the investigation can go no further.

Here is a hypothesis that could be formed from the question, "How does acid rain affect plant growth?"

Hypothesis: Acid rain causes plants to grow more slowly.

Notice that the hypothesis provides some specifics that lead to methods of testing. The hypothesis can also lead to predictions. A **prediction** is what you think will be the outcome of your experiment or data collection. Predictions are usually stated in an "if...then" format. For example, if meat is kept at room temperature, then it will spoil faster than meat kept in the refrigerator. More than one prediction can be made for a single hypothesis.

Here is a sample prediction for the acid rain hypothesis.

Prediction: If a plant is watered only with acid rain (which has a pH of 4), then the plant will grow at one-half its normal rate.

3. Test the Hypothesis After you have formed a hypothesis and made a prediction, it is time to test your hypothesis. There are different ways to test a hypothesis. Perhaps the most familiar way is by conducting a controlled experiment. A **controlled experiment** is an experiment that tests only one factor at a time. A controlled experiment has a **control group** and one or more experimental groups. All the factors for the control and **experimental groups** are the same except for one factor, which is called the **variable.** By changing only one factor (the variable), you can see the results of just that one change.

Sometimes, a controlled experiment is not possible due to the nature of the investigation. For example, stars are too far away, dinosaurs have been extinct for millions of years, and the Earth's core is surrounded by thousands of meters of rock. It would be difficult if not impossible to do controlled experiments on such things. Under these and many other circumstances, a hypothesis may be tested by making detailed observations. Taking measurements is one way of making observations.

4. Analyze the Results After you have completed your experiments, made your observations, and collected your data, you must analyze all the information you have gathered. Tables and graphs are often used in this step to organize the data.

5. Draw Conclusions Based on the analysis of your data, you should conclude whether your results support your hypothesis. If your hypothesis is supported, you (or others) might want to repeat the observations or experiments to verify your results. If your hypothesis is not supported by the data, you may have to check your procedure for errors. You may even have to reject your hypothesis and make a new one. If you cannot draw a conclusion from your results, you may have to try the investigation again or carry out further observations or experiments.

6. Communicate Results After any scientific investigation, you should report your results. By doing a written or oral report, you let others know what you have learned. They may want to repeat your investigation to see if they get the same results. Your report may even lead to another question, which in turn may lead to another investigation.

Water Wigglers

Purpose

Students develop a system of classification by examining living organisms from a natural water source.

Time Required

Three 45-minute class periods
Day 1: 45 minutes to collect water samples and make observations
Day 2: 45 minutes to examine organisms in different samples
Day 3: 45 minutes to classify the organisms

Lab Ratings

EASY ——————→ HARD

TEACHER PREP

STUDENT SET-UP

CONCEPT LEVEL

CLEAN UP

ADDITIONAL MATERIALS (PER CLASS)

- methyl cellulose or Detain™
- Various cultures (optional), such as *Paramecium, Euglena, Amoeba, Volvox, Stentor, Spirogyra*

Advance Preparation

Locate a nearby slow-moving or stationary body of water. Schedule your water collection on a day when water temperatures are moderate for your area, such as in late spring or early fall. Designate an area where students can store their water samples overnight.

Purchase a slowing agent, such as methyl cellulose or Detain™, from a biological supply company, and prepare a dilute solution according to the manufacturer's instructions. One week before the activity, have students collect small glass jars with lids, such as baby food jars. You may also use stoppered test tubes. Depression slides are preferred, but regular slides will also work.

Before the second day of class, check a sample of the pond water so that you will know what kinds of organisms students are likely to find. Set up a microscope station for each group. Number the stations. To ensure that students have a variety of organisms to compare, you may want to set up microscope stations with slides of pure cultures of microorganisms. See the Additional Materials box for suggested organisms. You may use a microprojector so students can make observations of the collected cultures and pure cultures as a class.

Provide a disposal receptacle for used cotton balls, plastic slides, and plastic cover slips. If glass slides and cover slips are used, provide a separate disposal container for them.

Safety Information

Do not permit horseplay near the water. Pond water may contain harmful organisms. Students should wash their hands thoroughly with soap and water after handling pond water.

To avoid transmission of eye infections, each student should clean the microscope eyepiece with an alcohol-moistened cotton ball after use. Students should **not** ingest the slowing agent. If microscopes use a mirror rather than a lamp, do not allow students to use sunlight as a light source; doing so can damage their eyes.

continued...

LIFE SCIENCE

Paula Sizemore
East Middle School
Salem, Michigan

Do not allow students to operate microscopes with damaged or frayed electrical cords or allow electrical cords to dangle from workstations. (You may want to secure the cords with tape to prevent tripping.) Provide paper towels, and instruct students to dry their hands and work areas before plugging in microscopes.

Teaching Strategies

This activity works best in groups of 2–3 students. Have students complete the lab *before* studying classification.

Day 1: Have students bring their ScienceLog to the collection site so they can sketch some of the things they see. As you approach the body of water, ask students what they expect to find. Then ask students to describe what life-forms they actually see in the water. If possible, have different groups collect their samples from different regions of the body of water, such as near the shore, in and out of vegetation, and offshore. Have students label their jar indicating the collection location. Store the water overnight at room temperature.

Day 2: Review with students the parts and operation of a microscope and the proper way to make a wet mount. Also show students how to disinfect the eyepiece after use. You may want to point out that a slide is a harsh environment for the pond organisms. If slides begin to dry out, students can add a drop of water from their culture. After all groups complete their observations at the first station, have them begin observing pure cultures at the numbered stations. After the activity, remind students to wash their hands. Have students pour their unused pond water into one larger container for easy disposal.

Day 3: Begin by asking students why we classify things. (*Accept all reasonable answers.*) Divide the class into groups, and have each group list foods they have eaten in the last few days. Next have students divide their list into different categories, such as drinks, desserts, and salty foods. Ask each group to justify their categories or groupings. Help students understand that organisms can also be classified according to characteristics.

Ask students to describe what they saw at each microscope station, and record their answers on the board. Students may observe algae (appearing green, bluish, or yellow) that do not propel themselves. When all the observations have been recorded, ask students to look for similarities among the organisms. List these on the board.

Have students group the organisms according to common characteristics, such as size, shape, color, appendages, or method of locomotion. Next have students name the groups and individual organisms based on their characteristics. (*Accept all reasonable answers.*) As an extension, you might have students develop a dichotomous key for identifying different kinds of water organisms.

Evaluation Strategies

For help evaluating this lab, see the Rubric for Performance Assessment and the Checklist for Self-Evaluation of Lesson in the *Assessment Checklists & Rubrics*. These resources are also available in the *Classroom Management CD-ROM*.

FIELD ACTIVITY

1 **STUDENT WORKSHEET**

DESIGN YOUR OWN

Water Wigglers

If you liked Sea Monkeys, you'll love our new Water Wiggler Zoo!

Call now, and you'll receive a critter zoo not visible with the naked eye! In this fabulous kit, you get a Super-Duper Microscope—complete with slides for viewing—and your Water Wiggler water droplets. But let's not stop there . . .

You can also classify your Water Wigglers into fun and interesting categories that you design! By the time you are done, you will have spent hours of fun developing your own critter classification. In the end, you will have your very own zoo! So order now! Your Water Wigglers await!

(Water Wigglers are not guaranteed to be in every water droplet.)

MATERIALS

- small glass jar with a lid
- 25 mL of pond water
- permanent marker
- plastic microscope slide
- plastic coverslip
- 2 disposable pipets
- sheet of white paper
- magnifying glass
- compound light microscope with 2 or 3 objectives
- slowing agent
- toothpick
- cotton balls
- rubbing alcohol

SCIENTIFIC **METHOD**

Ask a Question

How would you develop a classification system for organisms?

Make a Prediction

1. What will you observe in a drop of pond water?

_____

_____

Make Observations

2. **At the collection site:** Carefully fill a jar with water from a natural water source. Tightly close the lid.

3. Label the jar with the names of your group members. When you get back to class, store the jar in the area designated by your teacher.

4. **In class:** Each group will make one slide. Gently shake the jar, open the lid, and place the tip of a pipet in the water. Pinch the bulb and release it so that the pipet fills with water. Securely close the jar's lid. Squeeze a small drop of water onto the center of a slide. Carefully place a cover slip over the water droplet.

5. Place the slide over a sheet of white paper. Examine the water sample with the magnifying glass. What do you see? Record your observations in your ScienceLog. Take turns with all the members of your group.

6. Carefully place the slide on the microscope stage. Rotate the clips to hold the slide in place.

LIFE SCIENCE

Water Wigglers, continued

7. Rotate the low-powered objective over the cover slip. Look through the eyepiece and focus on the particles in the water. When you see a living organism, closely watch its movements. Make sure every group member makes observations.

8. If nothing appears on your slide, repeat steps 4–7.

9. Sometimes the organisms move too fast for you to see them clearly, but you can slow them down. Place the tip of a clean pipet in the slowing agent. Pinch and release the bulb to fill the pipet.

10. Carefully lift the cover slip, and squeeze a droplet of slowing agent onto the pond water. Mix gently with a toothpick. Cover the liquid with the cover slip. Look at the slide through the microscope.

11. In your ScienceLog, record the station number and the magnification, and draw each organism that you view through the eyepiece.

12. Describe how each organism moves through the liquid.

13. How many different kinds of organisms do you see? Identify the most and least numerous organisms.

14. After every group member has observed the sample under low power, rotate the higher-powered objective over the slide and repeat steps 11–13. Do you see more organisms? Do you see the same organisms in greater detail?

15. When your teacher gives you permission, move to another station and repeat steps 11–14 until your teacher tells you to stop.

16. Follow your teacher's instructions for cleaning up the lab area.

Analyze the Results

17. Your teacher will lead a discussion about the classification of organisms. When it is your turn, describe what you saw under the microscopes.

18. As a class, categorize the organisms. First divide the list of organisms into general groups. Then divide the groups into more specific subgroups.

19. As a group, name the organisms you sketched in your ScienceLog. Their names should reflect some identifying characteristic(s).

20. What features were most helpful in grouping the organisms?

_____

_____

_____

_____

_____

Critical Thinking

21. How would you change your classification system to be able to identify other kinds of organisms?

_____

_____

_____

_____

22. Study the picture below. Did you see any of these organisms? Circle the organisms you saw under the microscope.

Water Wigglers, continued

23. In a dictionary, look up the names of the organisms listed in the table below. What is the connection between an organism's name and its characteristics? For each organism in the table fill in the word root(s), meaning(s), and the connection between the name and the organism's characteristics.

Organism Names and Meanings

Name	Root(s)	Meaning	Connection
Actinophrys			
Amoeba			
Blepharisma			
Chlamydomonas			
Coleps			
Colpidium			
Cyclops			
Daphnia			
Euglena			
Paramecium			
Rotifer			
Stentor			
Stylonychia			
Synura			
Volvox			
Vorticella			

2 **TEACHER'S PREPARATORY GUIDE**

DISCOVERY LAB

Ditch's Brew

LIFE SCIENCE

Purpose

Students learn how microorganisms decompose organic material by making a compost pile.

Time Required

Four to six weeks to make compost
Day 1: 15 minutes to identify and sort compost materials
Day 2: 30 minutes to fill the compost bin and measure temperature
Weeks 1–6: 5 minutes each day to read the compost temperature and 15 minutes each week for 4–6 weeks to turn the compost

Lab Ratings

EASY ——————————→ HARD

TEACHER PREP
STUDENT SET-UP
CONCEPT LEVEL
CLEAN UP

ADDITIONAL MATERIALS

- measuring tape
- permanent marker
- 2 m stakes (4)
- hammer
- gardening gloves
- wire or plastic mesh, 0.5 × 7 m
- 16 metal twist ties
- white poster board (1 piece per class)

Advance Preparation

Each class will have one bin. Additional materials are available from most garden supply stores. To make a compost bin, measure a 1.5 × 1.5 m area. Mark each stake 1.5 m from the unpointed end, and hammer each stake into one corner of the measured area until the mark on the stake touches the ground. Wearing gardening gloves and long sleeves, secure the mesh around the bin by tying the mesh to each stake with metal twist ties. Indicate two collection areas near the bin. Make a tem-

perature chart and a temperature graph to post for each class. If your school is in an urban area, you may wish to use a plastic bin with holes poked in the lid. The dimensions of the bin should be about 90 × 60 × 60 cm. Plastic recycling bins with lids work well. This type of bin can be stored inside; placing it by a window away from students is best. If you choose to make the compost inside, the compost will need to be turned each week, and this lab will take 6–12 weeks to complete.

Safety Information

Students should wear gardening gloves and goggles while working near the bin. Compost can get very hot. Students should wear heat-resistant gloves when measuring the temperature. Students should shovel carefully and wash their hands and the outside of the plastic collection bags after handling compost.

Teaching Strategies

This activity is designed for the whole class to work on together. When the compost bin is full, insert the thermometer into the center of the pile. Each day, have 1–2 students from the class read the temperature, moisten the pile (if necessary), and record the temperature on the class chart and graph.

After students record their daily observations, date and staple one bag of compost beside the class chart to show the progress of the pile. Return the contents of the other bags to the pile.

Evaluation Strategies

For help evaluating this lab, see the Rubric for Performance Assessment in the *Assessment Checklists & Rubrics*. This rubric is also available in the *Classroom Management CD-ROM.*

CLASSROOM TESTED & APPROVED

Kenneth Creese
White Mountain Junior High
Rock Springs, Wyoming

FIELD ACTIVITY

2 STUDENT WORKSHEET

DISCOVERY LAB

Ditch's Brew

Double double, toil and trouble
Compost helps diminish the rubble!

Veggie scraps, some grass, and leaves
Give nitrogen that feeds our needs.
Wood chips, dry leaves, lint, and dust
Provide the carbon—that's a must!

Herbicides, plastic, ashes and meat—
don't use them for they're no treat.
Weeds, logs, and plants diseased
Are not what compost heaps will need.

Too much carbon won't break down,
Too much nitrogen stinks up the town
Equal parts of both, you see
Make the perfect recipe.

Compost adds organic stuff
So the soil has just enough.
Put your garden on a diet
Of healthy compost—won't you try it?

Double double, toil and trouble
Compost heaps eat up your rubble!

MATERIALS

- 8–10 resealable plastic bags
- shovel
- water hose connected to a spigot (one per class)
- heat-resistant gloves
- compost thermometer (one per class)

Objective

Compost a variety of materials to learn how different micro-organisms work together to break down organic matter.

Compost Contents 101

Decomposing organisms use the carbon and nitrogen in plants as nutrients. With the proper nutrients, the organisms will survive in a compost pile. You will collect materials to add to a compost pile. Find out what materials to collect by rereading the introduction and answering the questions below.

1. Which items can go into the compost pile?

_____

_____

_____

2. Which items cannot go into the compost pile?

_____

_____

_____

3. What is the perfect recipe for a compost pile?

_____

_____

_____

Ditch's Brew, continued

---

4. **At home:** Fill one plastic grocery bag with carbon-rich materials and another bag with nitrogen-rich materials. Bring the collected materials to class.

Pile It On!

5. Outside, place your carbon-rich materials in the area labeled "carbon" and your nitrogen-rich materials in the area labeled "nitrogen."

6. Pick out the coarse, bulky material, and place it at the bottom of the compost bin to allow air to circulate.

7. Fill the bin by alternating thin layers of materials from the carbon and nitrogen piles. Add layers until the bin is full. Congratulations! You have just made the perfect "brew" to encourage decomposers to break down organic matter.

Keep It Brewing!

8. Moisten the pile with water when needed.

9. **Each day:** Read the compost pile temperature, and turn the pile when necessary. Record the temperature of the compost pile in your ScienceLog.
   - If the temperature is below 60°C, do not turn the compost.
   - The pile should reach an average temperature of 60°C within the first few days. When the temperature becomes constant, remove the thermometer, and use a shovel to turn the pile, bringing fresh air to the microbes. Their numbers will multiply quickly, and the pile will reheat. Collect a compost sample from the center of the pile, and seal it in a plastic bag.

10. Examine the compost sample. How well has the compost broken down?

11. Review the information on page 10. In your ScienceLog, identify which phase of the cycle the compost is in and which decomposing organisms are at work in the pile.

12. In several days, the pile will reheat, but probably not to 60°C. After the temperature remains constant for 2–3 days, turn the pile with a shovel. As you turn the pile, move any uncomposted materials to the center of the pile. After turning the pile, repeat steps 10 and 11.

13. Repeat step 12 until the compost no longer heats up significantly. Finished compost should look dark, crumble easily, and have a fresh, earthy smell. If there are any portions of the pile that still need decomposing, move them to the center of the pile.

14. In your ScienceLog, write the "Story of the Ditch's Brew." Begin with the building of the pile on the first day, and describe the events and changes that occurred over the course of the lab. Be sure to include the temperature changes and specific observations.

Hot Stuff!

Composting takes advantage of natural cycles by which bacteria and fungi break down organic matter. Carbon dioxide, heat, and water are given off, and an organic end product called humus is produced. The method used in this lab is called hot composting because high temperatures speed up the natural processes. Ideally, compost materials go through a cycle of moderate-temperature and high-temperature phases. The chart below lists the basic processes and the most common microbes for each phase.

Phases of Composting

Moderate-temperature phase (28–40°C)	High-temperature phase (40–60°C)
• Simple substances break down. • Compost heats up as bacteria use nutrients. • Moderate-temperature microbes: **Bacillus** bacteria live in topsoil and help break down soluble compounds. They are visible with a microscope. **Molds** appear as gray or white fuzzy colonies on the surface of the pile. They help break down complex plant polymers.	• Complex substances break down. • Compost cools as it is turned and as nutrients are used up. • High-temperature microbes: **Thermus** bacteria predominate and help break down proteins, fats, and complex carbohydrates.
Both phases	
• **Fungi** appear in the outer compost layer. They break down organic matter that is too dry, acidic, tough, or too low in nitrogen for bacteria to break down. • **Actinomycetes** tend to appear in the outer 10–15 cm of the pile. They are most abundant toward the end of the composting process. Actinomycetes look like spider webs in the compost. They break down tough materials such as woody stems and bark. • **Invertebrates,** such as sow bugs, worms, and adult and larval insects, help break down materials into smaller pieces, aerate the pile, and transport microbes through the pile.	

Using Compost

When the compost is ready, your teacher may allow you to take some home. Use compost once or twice a year to enrich garden soil. Spread a 10 cm deep layer of compost over a garden area, and work it into the top 20 cm of soil. Ideally, the soil should sit for a few weeks before planting.

The Case of the Ravenous Radish

Purpose

Students grow radishes in crowded and uncrowded environments to determine how overpopulation affects plant growth.

Time Required

Three weeks to grow radishes
Day 1: 20 minutes to plant the seeds
Days 2–20: 5 minutes each school day to water and check the radishes
Day 21: 15 minutes to discuss the results

Lab Ratings

EASY ———————————→ HARD

TEACHER PREP
STUDENT SET-UP
CONCEPT LEVEL
CLEAN UP

Advance Preparation

Begin this activity two weeks before studying the chapters on plants so students can correlate the growth of their radishes with their studies. One week in advance, have students bring in plastic rectangular containers or tubs. Other alternatives to planters include plastic cups, tofu or yogurt containers, and milk containers with a portion cut away. If you have enough containers and storage space, you may wish to conduct this activity with the "crowded" and "uncrowded" environments in separate containers. Each group will need approximately 2 kg of potting soil to fill the group's box. Soak the seeds in water overnight to break down the seed coat. The seeds require an average of 8–10 hours of light each day. To ensure sufficient light, the growing area should be near a sunny window, below fluorescent growing lamps, or outside. Alternatively, you can use a Growlab™. If the growing area is inside, cover the area's surface.

Safety Information

Seeds are often coated with a fungicide. Students should not taste or ingest seeds. Have students wear disposable gloves when handling plants or seeds and avoid touching their hands to their face and eyes. Students should wash their hands thoroughly after contact with seeds, soil, or plants.

Teaching Strategies

This activity works best in groups of 4–6 students. Begin by asking students what they need in order to grow normally *(proper diet, exercise, water)*. Then ask them what plants need to grow normally *(light, water, soil, nutrients)*.

Students may be surprised at the differences between crowded and uncrowded radishes. Plants that have to compete for water and other nutrients appear to suffer from malnutrition. Students may also notice some leaf crowding, which indicates competition for sunlight. All plant processes, including growth, are fueled by sunlight. Sun-starved plants can suffer even more than plants subject to nutrient limitations.

Evaluation Strategies

For help evaluating this lab, see the Rubric for Performance Assessment and the Checklist for Self-Evaluation of Lesson in the *Assessment Checklists & Rubrics*. These resources are also available in the *Classroom Management CD-ROM*.

CLASSROOM TESTED & APPROVED

Elizabeth Rustad
Crane Junior High
Yuma, Arizona

ECOLAB

3 **STUDENT WORKSHEET**

DISCOVERY
LAB

The Case of the Ravenous Radish

The Industrial Radish Growers Association (IRGA) is mad. It is suing Ma Olson's Happy Radish Co-op for libel, slander, and defamation. Recently, Ma Olson ran an ad claiming that Co-op radishes are bigger, healthier, and tastier than those grown by the IRGA. The IRGA says there is nothing to support that claim.

Ma Olson, Co-op founder and owner, stands by her claim and says that the ad is true. The fields of the Co-op are much more spacious than IRGA farms, which grow "ravenous radishes" due to crowded conditions.

The IRGA is suing Ma Olson for damage to its reputation and to its business. It is up to you, the jury, to decide if Ma Olson's claims are true and to close the Case of the Ravenous Radish.

MATERIALS

- disposable gloves
- plastic rectangular containers
- potting soil
- masking tape
- metric ruler
- pencil
- 48 radish seeds
- permanent marker
- large plastic cup
- water
- spray bottle

 Ask a Question

SCIENTIFIC METHOD

How does overpopulation affect the growth and development of radish plants?

Make a Prediction

1. How does overpopulation affect the growth and development of radish plants?

_____

_____

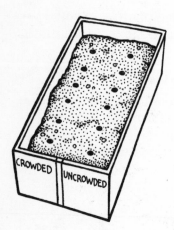

Conduct an Experiment

2. Fill the container with potting soil up to 3 cm from the top. Do not pack the soil. Holes in the soil trap water.

3. Divide the container in half by placing a line down the center of its side with masking tape as shown. Label one side "crowded" and the other side "uncrowded." Label the container with the names of your group members.

4. With the eraser end of a pencil, poke two rows of six holes, 1 cm deep, into the soil, as shown. Be sure the holes are spaced about 3 cm apart and at least 3 cm away from the sides of the container.

5. On the "crowded" side of the container, place six radish seeds in each hole. Cover the holes with soil.

6. On the "uncrowded" side of the container, place two radish seeds in each hole. Cover the holes with soil.

7. Fill a cup with water, and pour half of the water over the seeds in each side of the container. Place the container in the area that your teacher has set aside.

The Case of the Ravenous Radish, continued

SAFETY ALERT!

Be sure to wash your hands thoroughly after working with the soil.

8. Mist your seeds every day using a spray bottle filled with water.

Collect Data

9. After your radishes have grown for about 20 days, make a table in your ScienceLog like the one below.

Radish Growth Observations

Crowded radishes	Width	Other observations	Uncrowded radishes	Width	Other observations
1	2 mm		1	20 mm	
2	4 mm		2	40 mm	

10. Gently remove the radishes from each hole on the "uncrowded" side of the box. With a metric ruler, measure the width of each radish, and record the width along with other observations in your ScienceLog.

11. Repeat step 11 for the "crowded" side of the box.

Analyze the Results

12. Was your prediction correct? Explain.

_____

_____

13. What factor(s) appear to have affected the radishes' growth rates the most?

_____

_____

_____

Draw Conclusions

14. How could space affect the supply of nutrients to a plant?

_____

_____

_____

_____

_____

Recycle! Make Your Own Paper

Purpose

Students recycle used paper to create new paper and learn about the conservation of renewable resources.

Time Required

Two 45-minute class periods

Lab Ratings

EASY ——————————→ HARD

TEACHER PREP   ▲▲▲

STUDENT SET-UP   ▲▲

CONCEPT LEVEL   ▲

CLEAN UP   ▲▲▲

ADDITIONAL MATERIALS (PER CLASS)

- scrap paper (copier, laser, and wrapping paper), old maps, and card stock
- cup of dryer lint
- blender
- cup of flower petals or leaves
- water pitcher

- colored thread
- waste pail
- cotton balls
- fruits, vegetables, and spices
- tarp
- coffee filters
- extra cups
- 5 mL teaspoon

Advance Preparation

A few days before the activity, ask students to collect dryer lint, flower petals, leaves, colored thread, and scrap paper. Heavy paper yields better results than newspaper or magazines. Ask each student to bring an old hand towel for the activity. Have extras available. Sort the materials by color into piles. Cover each group's work surface, and set up a decoration station and a "slurry" station. The decoration station contains cotton balls, extra cups, and the sorted materials. The slurry station contains a blender and a water pitcher; position this station near a faucet. Designate a disposal receptacle for unused slurry. Select a flat area to dry the paper. Construct and test a papermaker before class to use as a model. You may substitute lab trays for pans.

Select fresh fruits, vegetables, and dried spices to produce several pigments for day 2. Dice or grate fruits and vegetables. Combine half a cup of water and 1 cup of diced fruit or vegetables in a blender. Pulse the blender until the mixture is smooth. Strain through a coffee filter into a large cup. Rinse the blender well between uses.

Safety Information

Students should not operate the blender. Keep the blender cord and plug dry. Keep the blender closed while in operation.

Teaching Strategies

This activity works best in groups of 2–4 students. Begin by discussing resources that are renewed by biological processes, such as trees, oxygen, nitrogen, and clean water. Ask why we need to consider conserving resources that are renewed naturally. *(Resources may have a long replenishment time, they may be depleted over time, or the process whereby the resource is renewed may be disrupted.)* Discuss how paper is produced commercially. Typically, trees are ground to a pulp. Wood pulp is bleached, treated, and sprayed into sheets.

Demonstrate how to use the papermaker. If time allows, students can make paper in various shapes by taping different shapes on the nylon.

Evaluation Strategies

For help evaluating this lab, see the Checklist for Teacher Evaluation of Lesson in the *Assessment Checklists & Rubrics*. This checklist is also available in the *Classroom Management CD-ROM*.

CLASSROOM TESTED & APPROVED

Christopher Wood
Western Rockingham
Middle School
Madison, North Carolina

4 **STUDENT WORKSHEET**

Recycle! Make Your Own Paper

Being an artist isn't easy, especially an artist who uses only one medium. Your medium is paper. Paper is manufactured especially for you from a select group of trees. From the special paper, you have constructed colossal collages, ominous origami, and stupendous sculptures that are famous the world over.

Lately, your work has been boring and uninspired, and people are beginning to call you the Tree Taker instead of an artistic genius. To get back in their good graces, you need something different—something that will really WOW them.

Suddenly, you get an idea. Why not create handmade paper from used materials? By collecting old fibers, used paper, and plants of various colors, you can mix materials together to create truly unique sheets of paper.

Imagine the colors! Imagine the textures! Imagine all the trees that will be spared! You will go from being the Tree Taker to papermaker extraordinaire!

LIFE SCIENCE ▲▲▲

MATERIALS

- embroidery hoop 20–26 cm in diameter
- knee-high nylon stocking; no runs
- duct tape
- scissors
- 5 mL of cornstarch
- 500 mL cup
- scrap paper
- water
- roasting pan at least 10 cm deep
- long-handled spoon
- cotton balls
- 3–4 towels
- 3–4 sponges

Objective

Recycle old paper to make new paper.

Tear It Up!

1. Separate the inner and outer parts of the embroidery hoop.

2. Put the inner hoop into the stocking. Avoid ripping the stocking!

3. When the hoop is completely covered, replace the outer hoop, and tighten the screw so that it fits snugly.

4. Place four pieces of duct tape along the edges of the hoop so that the center forms a rectangle, as shown. Congratulations! You have constructed a *papermaker*.

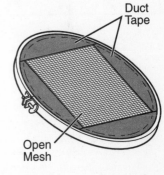
Duct Tape

Open Mesh

5. Add 5 mL of cornstarch to a 500 mL cup. Adding the cornstarch to the paper will prevent ink from bleeding. Shred paper into small pieces, and tightly pack it to fill the cup.

6. At the slurry station, carefully add 1 L of water to the blender. Add half of the contents of the cup to the blender, and securely place the lid on the blender. Your teacher will blend the mixture until it forms a smooth pulp called slurry. Carefully pour the pulp into a pan.

7. Repeat step 6 using the remainder of the cup's contents.

8. At the decoration station, choose various items to decorate your paper. Add them to your slurry, and blend the mixture with a spoon.

Recycle! Make Your Own Paper, continued

9. Separate the fibers of several cotton balls, and add them to the slurry to strengthen the paper. Stir the fibers into the slurry with a spoon until they are evenly distributed.

10. Use tape to label a towel with your name. Place the unfolded towel beside the pan. Hold the papermaker tape-side up. Scoop the papermaker into the slurry, and let it rest for a few minutes on the bottom of the pan. Fibers will settle on top of the papermaker.

11. Without tilting the papermaker, slowly lift it out of the pan. Let the water drain into the pan.

12. When the papermaker stops dripping, carefully flip it onto the towel so that the new paper lies between the papermaker and the towel.

13. Gently press on the nylon with the sponge, and rub the sponge along the back of the mesh to absorb the water. Remove the excess water to strengthen your paper and to help it dry quickly. When your sponge is full of water, wring the water into the pan.

14. Repeat step 13 until you can no longer remove water from the paper.

HELPFUL HINT

If the paper rips, press the edges together with wet fingers.

15. Carefully lift the papermaker off of your new paper sheet. Gently lift the towel with the paper on it, and move it to the drying area. Congratulations! You have made your own paper!

16. Repeat steps 10–15 for each group member.

17. Discard any unused pulp mixture into a compost pile or a container that your teacher has provided. **Do not** pour the slurry down the drain. Slurry clogs pipes.

Analyzing Your Papermaking Process

18. Paper is made of dried plant fibers. What happened to the fibers in each of the steps you followed?

The Fate of the Fibers

Action	What happened to the fibers?
Step 1: Added water and blended the scrap paper	
Step 2: Lifted the papermaker from the pan	
Step 3: Dried the paper	

19. How could this lab change to better conserve resources?

_____

_____

_____

_____

20. How does recycling paper help the environment?

_____

_____

_____

_____

_____

_____

DECORATING MATERIALS

- 3–4 sponges
- scissors
- bowl
- various natural pigments
- large feather
- water
- disposable gloves

HELPFUL HINT

Boiling the natural ingredients below left in water will make the corresponding pigment colors:

turmeric	orange
marigolds	yellow
onion peels	yellow
blueberries	blue
cranberries	red
raspberries	pink

21. How can making paper from fibrous, nonwoody plants help the environment?

_____

_____

_____

_____

_____

Be an Artist!

22. Turn your paper into a work of art, such as a greeting card. Follow the steps below to add a little color to your paper. Your teacher will provide pigments made from fruits, vegetables, or spices.

23. Cut sponges into different shapes to form stamps.

24. Dip a stamp into a pigment. Press the stamp onto your sheet of paper. **Rinse your sponge before dipping it in another color.**

25. Dip the tip of a feather into the pigment, and use it as a pen to write a message or sign your masterpiece!

26. Let the pigment dry before handling your art.

LIFE SCIENCE

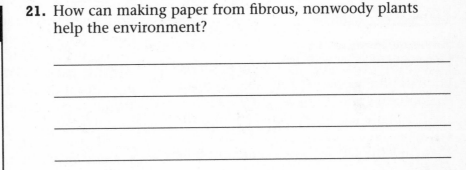

Survival Is Just a Roll of the Dice

Cooperative Learning Activity

Group size: 2–3 students

Group goal: Model the changing population of a wolf pack to learn about the factors that can affect population size and survival rate.

Positive interdependence: Each group member should choose a role, such as recorder, consequence reader, and wolf counter.

Individual accountability: After the game, each group member should be able to critically analyze his or her results.

Time Required

One 45-minute class period

Lab Ratings

EASY ——————→ HARD

TEACHER PREP 🝢🝢

STUDENT SET-UP 🝢

CONCEPT LEVEL 🝢🝢

CLEAN UP 🝢

Advance Preparation

Dice must have numbers 1–6 only. Make enough photocopies of the table on page 21 for each group to have two. Provide reading materials for students about different types of wolves. Have a map handy so that students can see where different types of wolves live.

Safety Information

Beans or dice that fall on the floor are hazardous.

Teaching Strategies

Begin by discussing with students their role in an ecosystem. Ask students to list factors that may limit human population. Then ask students to list factors that might limit the population size of other animals. Compare the two lists, and ask students to explain why one population might become larger than another. Point out that one species can endanger the existence of another by overpopulating a shared habitat and using up limited resources.

Several types of wolves have been placed on the endangered species list. Have students read materials about different types of wolves. The National Wildlife Federation is a good source of information. Then ask students the following questions: "Where do different types of wolves live?" "How many wolves are usually in a pack?" "What happens to maturing pups if the pack gets too large?" "What happens to the pack during a food shortage?"

After the activity, you may combine students' game results to make graphs for Games 1 and 2. This will help students grasp the long-term aspects of the effects of human interference on animal populations.

Evaluation Strategies

For help evaluating this lab, see the Rubric for Performance Assessment in the *Assessment Checklists & Rubrics*. This rubric is also available in the *Classroom Management CD-ROM*.

CLASSROOM TESTED & APPROVED

Paula Sizemore
East Middle School
Salem, Michigan

MAKING MODELS

▶ LIFE SCIENCE

Survival Is Just a Roll of the Dice

It is twenty years in the future . . .

You and your colleagues have just discovered a pack of gray wolves—wolves that were believed to be extinct!

In the late 1990s, gray wolves were on the endangered species list. Great efforts were made to protect gray wolves: they were moved to areas where they were protected, and hunters who shot wolves were heavily fined. Ranchers were compensated for livestock that wolves killed.

As the gray wolf population grew, the wolves were removed from the endangered species list. Biologists continued to monitor the populations by tracking some wolves with radio transmitter collars. However, without the protection of the Endangered Species Act, the wolves faced too many challenges and died out.

Or did they? Your team has just spotted a pack of gray wolves! Back at camp, you develop a model of this wolf pack's population and use it to determine what must be done to make sure this pack survives.

MATERIALS

- 2 dice
- cup of beans
- pencil

SAFETY ALERT!

Beans or dice on the floor are hazardous.

Objective

Model the changing population of a wolf pack. The team with the largest pack at the end of 15 years wins.

A Game Called Life

1. Place eight beans on the table. Two beans represent adult wolves, and the other six represent a litter of pups.

2. Roll the dice to represent the passage of 6 months. Count the dice, and read what happens to your pack on the Game 1 table (page 20). Fill in the Record-Keeping Table on page 21. Adjust the number of beans accordingly.

3. Repeat step 2 for the second 6 months. Count the number of wolves you have in your pack, and fill in the rest of year 1 on the table.

4. **Reproduction:** After year 1, add six pups at the beginning of each year unless a food shortage occurred the previous year. Adjust the number of beans accordingly.

5. **Maturation:** When the pack gets too large, the mature pups leave. Subtract six wolves if your pack has more than nine wolves. Adjust the number of beans accordingly, and record the pack total in the last column of the table.

6. Repeat steps 2–5 until you complete 15 years of play or until your pack dies out, whichever comes first.

_____

Survival Is Just a Roll of the Dice, continued

Game 1: With Human Interference

If you roll:	You:	Reason:
Double 2s, 3s, 4s, or 5s	subtract 3	high pup mortality rate; three pups die
2	divide by 2 (round down)	disease kills half the pack
3	subtract 1	one pup dies
4 (1+3)	subtract 1	one wolf dies of natural causes
5	subtract 2	hunter kills two wolves
6 (2+4 or 1+5)	make no changes	pack lives well for 6 months
7	make no changes	pack lives well for 6 months
8 (2+6 or 3+5)	follow step 6	food shortage occurs
9	subtract 2	rancher kills two wolves
10 (4+6)	subtract 1	wolf hit by car
11	subtract 1	wolf killed in an attack by another wolf pack
12	add 1	new wolf joins pack

7. Play this game again, only this time use the Game 2 table below. Record your answers on the table provided.

Game 2: Without Human Interference

If you roll:	You:	Reason:
Double 2s, 3s, 4s, or 5s	add 3	high pup mortality rate; three pups die
2	divide by 2 (round down)	disease kills half the pack
3	follow step 6	food shortage occurs
4 (1+3)	subtract 1	one wolf dies of natural causes
5	subtract 1	wolf killed in an attack by another wolf pack
6 (2+4 or 1+5)	make no changes	pack lives well for 6 months
7	make no changes	pack lives well for 6 months
8 (2+6 or 3+5)	subtract 1	one pup dies
9	make no changes	pack lives well for 6 months
10 (4+6)	subtract 1	wolf killed in an attack by another wolf pack
11	make no changes	pack lives well for 6 months
12	add 1	new wolf joins pack

Record-Keeping Table

Year	Last year's total	Add a litter (+6)	First 6 months Reason	First 6 months Affect on pack	Second 6 months Reason	Second 6 months Affect on pack	Pack subtotal	Subtract matured pups?	Total pack for year
1	2	+6						NO	
2								NO	
3									
4									
5									
6									
7									
8									
9									
10									
11									
12									
13									
14									
15									

LIFE SCIENCE

Analyze the Results

8. Did any team's pack die in either of the games? How?

_____

_____

_____

Critical Thinking

9. Considering what you learned in the game, could wolves overpopulate without human interference? Explain.

_____

_____

_____

_____

10. How could the disappearance of wolves from their ecosystem affect the populations of other species?

_____

_____

_____

_____

11. Do you feel this game accurately modeled the changing population of a wolf pack? Explain your answer.

_____

_____

_____

_____

12. What could be done to improve the potential survival of your pack?

_____

_____

_____

6 | **TEACHER'S PREPARATORY GUIDE**

Bacteria on Venus?

Purpose

Students study the effects of added nutrients on microbial succession by assembling and comparing enriched and control microbial communities.

Time Required

Two 45-minute class periods to explain and set up the lab and 10 minutes each week for 6 weeks to record observations

Lab Ratings

EASY ————————→ HARD

TEACHER PREP

STUDENT SET-UP

CONCEPT LEVEL

CLEAN UP

ADDITIONAL MATERIALS

- 1.9 L ($\frac{1}{2}$ gal) plastic milk jugs with lids (1 per group)
- craft knife
- duct tape
- disinfectant

Advance Preparation

One week before the activity, collect clear, 0.5 L plastic bottles with screw-on caps. Remove the labels. Select a natural body of salt or fresh water for collecting mud samples. The night before the lab, boil the eggs for 8 minutes. Cut a newspaper page into eight pieces. Construct a mud scoop for each group by carefully cutting off the bottom of a milk jug with a craft knife, as shown. Tape the lids to the jugs, and label the halfway point on the scoops. Cover all work areas in the classroom.

Designate an area where bottles of mud can be stored for 6 weeks.

Safety Information

Do not permit horseplay near the water. Students should wear neoprene gloves and an apron. Remind students not to touch their face or rub their skin, eyes, nose, or mouth. Students should disinfectant their work area and wash their hands thoroughly before and after the setup. Instruct students not to open their bottle once sealed. Treat all growth in bottles as pathogens. Dispose of all bottles as you would a biohazard.

Teaching Strategies

This activity works best in groups of 2–4 students. You could set up outside to minimize the cleanup. Use the lab results to discuss the cycle students observed:

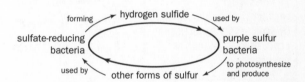

It is possible for bacteria to live in extreme environments. Certain types of bacteria have been found living in the hot springs at Yellowstone Park and at depths of 2,500 m in the ocean.

Evaluation Strategies

For help evaluating this lab, see the Rubric for Experiments in the *Assessment Checklists & Rubrics*. This rubric is also available in the *Classroom Management CD-ROM*.

Elizabeth Rustad
Crane Junior High
Yuma, Arizona

LIFE SCIENCE

FIELD ACTIVITY

6 **STUDENT WORKSHEET**

DISCOVERY LAB

Bacteria on Venus?

We hope you can settle a debate. Is it possible for bacteria to exist on Venus?

The surface of Venus is extremely hot and dry. At a scorching 462°C, it is hotter than most ovens! Because water boils at 100°C, the planet's surface is too hot for any moisture to remain as a liquid. It's doubtful that bacteria could live there.

The lower atmosphere of Venus is extremely hot and composed mostly of carbon dioxide along with traces of nitrogen and water vapor. The upper atmosphere of Venus is filled with thick clouds of sulfuric acid and averages a cool 13°C (55°F). Perhaps bacteria could live there.

We would like you to investigate bacteria in a closed system. Use environmentally friendly materials. For example, egg yolks are a nonhazardous source of sulfur. Because there is a high level of carbon dioxide in the atmosphere of Venus, add carbon to your experiment. Remember to seal your experiment so that no air or additional bacteria can enter. Please contact me with your results as soon as possible. Thank you.

Dr. Mike Robe

USEFUL TERM

succession
replacement over time of species in a natural community by other species

MATERIALS

- 0.5 L clear plastic bottles with caps (2)
- metric ruler
- permanent marker
- neoprene gloves
- mud scoop
- 1 L of mud
- panel of newspaper
- hard-boiled egg
- large funnel
- set of colored pencils

SCIENTIFIC METHOD

Ask a Question
Is it possible for microbes to live on Venus?

Make a Prediction

1. Do you think that bacteria could live on Venus? Explain.

   _____

   _____

   _____

Conduct an Experiment

2. **In class:** Measure 2 cm from the top of each bottle. Mark and label this point "full." Label one bottle "enriched," and label the other bottle "not enriched." Label both bottles with the names of your group members.

3. **At the collection site:** Fill the scoop to the halfway mark with mud from a naturally occurring water source.

4. **In class:** Pour the mud onto a covered workspace. Remove any hard lumps, twigs, rocks, and other large particles from the mud and discard. Separate the mud into two equal piles.

Bacteria on Venus? continued

LIFE SCIENCE

SAFETY ALERT!

- Wear neoprene gloves and an apron. Do not touch your face or rub your skin, eyes, nose, or mouth.
- After the activity, clean your work area with disinfectant.
- Dispose of materials as instructed by your teacher, and wash your hands thoroughly.

HELPFUL HINT

Do not open the bottles during the experiment or your results may be negatively affected.

5. Shred the newspaper, a source of carbon, into small pieces, and add a handful to one pile of mud. To add sulfur, crush the egg shell, and crumble the white and yolk into the same pile of mud. Mix well.

6. Use the funnel to carefully add the plain mud to the bottle labeled "not enriched." Use the funnel to carefully add the nutrient-enriched mud to the bottle labeled "enriched."

7. Cap each bottle tightly. Place your bottles in an area where they will receive indirect sunlight.

8. Make a chart in your ScienceLog like the one below. Use colored pencils to sketch the contents of each bottle in your ScienceLog at least once a week for 6 weeks. Date each entry, compare the bottles, and comment on anything that surprises you.

Bottle Bacteria Data

Week	Date	Bottle with nutrients	Bottle without nutrients	Comments
1				
2				

Analyze the Results

9. When did each of the following types of microbes appear?

   Green clumps: algae _____

   Black spots: sulfate-reducing bacteria _____

   Reddish purple spots: purple sulfur bacteria _____

   Rust-colored areas: purple nonsulfur bacteria _____

10. In which bottle did the contents change more slowly?

    _____

    _____

    _____

11. What evidence of succession did you see?

    _____

    _____

    _____

Bacteria on Venus? continued

---

12. What could have caused the succession in your bottle?

_____

_____

_____

_____

Draw Conclusions

13. Could sulfur-eating bacteria live in the atmosphere of Venus? Explain your answer.

_____

_____

_____

_____

_____

_____

_____

_____

_____

_____

Going Further

Believe it or not, the bacteria in your bottles can recycle old tires! Heat or chemical processing of rubber releases hazardous substances into the environment. But scientists have discovered that the types of bacteria you observed eat the sulfur in tires, breaking them down. The broken-down rubber can be made into new rubber tires that work as well as the original tires. The entire process is completely safe for the environment!

Find out how used tires are disposed of in your community. Write a letter to a recycling plant or to a local landfill explaining the benefits of recycling tires with bacteria.

DISCOVERY LAB

Biome Adventure Travel

LIFE SCIENCE

Cooperative Learning Activity

Group size: 3–4 students

Group goal: Research the features of biomes, and present an adventure-travel advertising campaign to reinforce and broaden knowledge about biomes.

Positive interdependence: Each group member should choose a role, such as research coordinator, recorder, discussion leader, or presentation coordinator.

Individual accountability: After the activity, students should be able to give detailed answers to questions regarding biomes.

Time Required

Two 45-minute class periods, depending on the depth of the project and accessibility of information. You may wish to assign the research portion of this project as homework.

Lab Ratings

EASY ———————→ HARD

TEACHER PREP

STUDENT SET-UP

CONCEPT LEVEL

CLEAN UP

Advance Preparation

One week before doing this activity, ask students to bring in travel and nature magazines, such as *National Geographic*. Be sure students understand that the magazines will not be returned. Assemble reference materials related to biomes, or arrange to use the library or Internet on the day of the activity. Provide each student with a copy of a world map.

Safety Information

Students should handle scissors with care.

Teaching Strategies

Before the activity, review the world's major biomes and their features.

Ask students where they would like to visit. What is it about a particular area that interests them? List these locations on the board. Ask students to categorize each location by biome type.

Students can use encyclopedias, almanacs, and the Internet to research their biomes and travel destinations. Suggest that students illustrate their brochures with a world map indicating each trip destination. Students can color their biomes and destinations on the map. Encourage students to bring in items such as feathers, leaves, and shells to add to their posters. If time allows, each group can pitch their advertising campaign to the class, and the class can then vote on the most effective campaign. Otherwise, groups can present their campaigns to one another. Display student posters and brochures after the activity.

Evaluation Strategies

For help evaluating this lab, see the Rubric for Reports and Presentations and the Checklist for Group Evaluation of a Cooperative Group Activity in the *Assessment Checklists & Rubrics*. These resources are also available in the *Classroom Management CD-ROM*.

CLASSROOM TESTED & APPROVED

Paula Sizemore
East Middle School
Salem, Michigan

Name _____ Date _____ Class _____

ECOLAB

7 **STUDENT WORKSHEET**

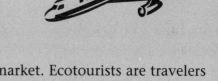

DISCOVERY LAB

Biome Adventure Travel

Earth Adventures Travel Agency

U R G E N T   M E M O

To: All Staff
From: E. Cotore, Marketing Manager

Subject: Travel Package Concept

The hottest market in the travel biz is the ecotourism market. Ecotourists are travelers who visit natural areas while taking care not to damage the habitats they visit. To serve this market, we want to be the first to offer exciting tours to the world's major biomes.

  Your assignment is to design and advertise a biome-adventure tour that takes travelers to at least four places around the globe. All of the tour destinations must belong to the same biome. For example, if you are designing a desert-biome tour, include visits to four or more deserts in different parts of the world. After you plan the tour, create an advertising campaign to promote the tour. Good luck!

MATERIALS

- world almanac and other geographical reference books
- travel magazines with photographs
- construction paper
- scissors
- butcher paper
- glue
- metric ruler
- colored markers
- map or globe

Objective

Learn about a particular biome by preparing a tour poster and a brochure.

Procedure

1. As a group, select a biome to research. Write the name of the biome below.

   We will research _____ **biome.**

2. Choose at least four tour destinations within that biome, and write them below.

   _____

   _____

3. Research each destination. Use what you learn to create a tour brochure with an attractive design in order to persuade travelers to visit these destinations. Include practical information for the traveler, such as the following:
   - expected temperatures and rainfall in different seasons
   - native plants and animals
   - ecological, historical, and cultural points of interest
   - native foods
   - adaptations to the biome by the local people, and use of local materials in crafts

28 HOLT SCIENCE AND TECHNOLOGY

Biome Adventure Travel, continued

4. Advertise your biome adventure with an original travel poster. Use illustrations and pictures to show features common to all of the destinations on your biome tour. Also include pictures of particular features for each place on the trip.

5. What characteristics are common to all of the destinations on your tour?

_____

_____

_____

_____

_____

6. Although all of your destinations belong to the same biome, they differ in several ways. Describe the differences between your tour destinations.

_____

_____

_____

_____

_____

_____

_____

7. Present your tour to another group. Use the poster and brochure to strengthen your sales pitch. Then pretend you are a tourist and listen as the other group tries to pitch their tour to you. Ask questions, and voice any concerns you may have. In your ScienceLog, list at least five things you learned from the other group's sales pitch about their biome.

LIFE SCIENCE

Biome Adventure Travel, continued

Analyze the Results

8. Would you like to tour the areas the other group advertised? Explain your answer.

_____

_____

_____

_____

_____

_____

9. How are biomes arranged around the globe? Explain your answer.

_____

_____

_____

_____

_____

_____

_____

_____

10. Discuss any exceptions to this basic pattern.

_____

_____

_____

_____

_____

_____

_____

_____

A Filter with Culture

LIFE SCIENCE

Purpose

Students construct simple filters to find the best method for cleaning water.

Time Required

Two 45-minute class periods

Lab Ratings

EASY ———————————→ HARD

TEACHER PREP

STUDENT SET-UP

CONCEPT LEVEL

CLEAN UP

ADDITIONAL MATERIALS

- 16.06 g of $KMnO_4$ (potassium permanganate)
- distilled water
- 1 L graduated container
- stirring rod
- 10 mL graduated cylinder
- 500 mL beaker

Advance Preparation

Ask students to collect small, clear glass jars with lids. Purchase activated carbon granules and potassium permanganate from a chemical supply house. Although you may use a regular funnel instead of a Buchner funnel, the water will take longer to filter. Use baker's yeast before it expires.

To make a 0.1016 M solution of $KMnO_4$ (potassium permanganate), place 16.06 g of $KMnO_4$ in a 1 L graduated container. Add enough distilled water while stirring to dissolve the solids. Add more water until the total volume is 1 L. Make the polluted water by placing 5 mL of 0.1016 M $KMnO_4$ solution in a 500 mL beaker and filling the beaker to the 500 mL mark with distilled water. Each group will need about 0.5–1.0 L of polluted water, depending on the size of the filter.

Safety Information

Instruct students not to drink any water from this lab. Avoid breathing activated carbon dust. Wear gloves while handling the polluted water.

Teaching Strategies

This activity works best with groups of 3–5 students. Begin the activity by discussing the variety of water pollutants, the potential sources of these pollutants, the consequences of pollution to humans and natural systems, and the different treatment methods required by different pollutants. Many water-filtration systems use an activated carbon bed like the one that will be tested.

After the activity, explain how the filters work. Yeast, as well as some bacteria, use heavy metals and toxic organic compounds as nutrient sources. Two considerations in using microbes are that great quantities must be used and that the microbes become solid toxic waste that must be disposed of. In areas with high levels of sodium or calcium in the water system, an ion exchanger like activated carbon can remove all metals from the water.

Students may be interested to know that the combination-filtration technique was developed by Elizabeth Philip as a high-school science-fair project. Her analysis showed that this method removes 99 percent of pollutants from the water.

Evaluation Strategies

For help evaluating this lab, see the Rubric for Performance Assessment in the *Assessment Checklists & Rubrics*.

This rubric is also available in the *Classroom Management CD-ROM.*

CLASSROOM TESTED & APPROVED

Elizabeth Rustad
Crane Junior High
Yuma, Arizona

ECOLAB
8 STUDENT WORKSHEET

DISCOVERY LAB

A Filter with Culture

The tiny town of Sweetwater is famous for its tasty, clean water and simple way of life. Tourists travel from hundreds of miles around just to sip the town's pure and refreshing water.

Last night a truck crashed, spilling a toxic chemical into Sweetwater's reservoir. Mayor H. Tuwo has declared a health emergency. Until the water is purified, residents will have no drinking water and farmers will have no water for their crops and animals. The tourists are leaving, and the residents may soon follow.

The town needs a fast and effective remedy. Mayor Tuwo has heard of your water-purification experiments with yeast. He has asked you to design a simple filtration system to remove the toxin from the town's water supply. Work quickly, or soon the town's name will be Dry Gulch!

MATERIALS

- coffee filters
- scissors
- 40 mL polypropylene Büchner funnel
- 500 mL beaker
- 40 g of activated carbon granules
- metric ruler
- tap water
- protective gloves
- 500 mL of polluted water
- 4 glass jars with lids
- permanent marker
- baker's yeast

SAFETY ALERT!

Wear protective gloves when handling the polluted water. Do not drink any water from this activity.

SCIENTIFIC **METHOD**

Ask A Question
Which simple filter works most effectively to remove a sample pollutant from water?

Make a Prediction

1. You will investigate the effectiveness of three filters: charcoal, yeast, and yeast with charcoal. Which filter do you think will be most effective?

   I think the _____ filter will be most effective.

Conduct an Experiment—Part 1: Test a Carbon Filter

2. **Day 1:** Trim seven coffee filters to fit inside the Büchner funnel. Place one filter inside the funnel.

3. Set the funnel over the beaker. Pack the carbon 1.25 cm high into the funnel. Place a second filter over the carbon.

4. Carefully pour in 250 mL of tap water to wet the activated carbon bed. After 5 minutes, discard the water that passed through the activated carbon bed.

5. Pour 100 mL of polluted water into an empty jar, screw on the lid, and label this jar "polluted water." Describe the polluted water.

   _____

   _____

6. Pour 100 mL of the polluted water into the activated carbon filter. Describe the water after it has passed through the carbon filter.

   _____

   _____

7. Pour some of the filtered water into a clean jar. Seal the jar, and label it "carbon-filtered water." Rinse the beaker.

8. Discard the filters and the charcoal. Rinse the funnel, and set it over the beaker.

Part 2: Test a Yeast Filter

9. Place a clean filter inside the funnel. Pour enough baker's yeast into the filter to form a layer 1.25 cm deep.

10. Carefully pour in 250 mL of tap water over the yeast to wet the yeast bed. After 5 minutes, discard the water that passed through the yeast bed.

11. Place a second filter on top of the yeast bed. Carefully pour 100 mL of polluted water into your yeast filter. Describe the water after it has passed through the filter.

_____

_____

12. **Day 2:** Pour the filtered water into a clean, empty jar. Seal the jar, and label it "yeast-filtered water." Rinse the beaker.

13. Discard the filters and yeast. Rinse the funnel, and set it over the beaker.

Part 3: Test a Combination Filter

14. Place a clean filter inside the funnel. Pack activated carbon 1.25 cm deep in the funnel. Place a second filter on top of the activated carbon.

15. Pour approximately 250 mL (enough to wet the activated carbon layer) of tap water through the activated carbon filter.

16. Pour enough baker's yeast to form a layer 1.25 cm deep above the activated carbon filter.

17. Place the third filter on top of the yeast bed. Pour approximately 250 mL (enough to wet the yeast bed) of tap water through the yeast bed. After 5 minutes, discard the water that passed through the carbon and yeast beds.

18. Carefully pour 100 mL of polluted water into the yeast filter. Describe the water after it has passed through the filter.

_____

19. Pour some of the filtered water into a clean, empty jar. Seal the jar, and label it "combination-filtered water."

LIFE SCIENCE

A Filter with Culture, continued

Analyze the Results

20. Compare the water samples in the three jars. Was your prediction correct? Explain your answer.

_____

_____

_____

_____

_____

HELPFUL HINT

After the activity, you may discard the yeast in a trash container.

21. List two advantages of using yeast and activated carbon to clean water.

_____

_____

_____

Draw Conclusions

22. Which filter would you recommend to the mayor of Sweetwater? Explain your answer.

_____

_____

_____

_____

Critical Thinking

23. How could the town use this filtering method to process all the water in the reservoir?

_____

_____

_____

_____

_____

DISCOVERY LAB

There's Something in the Air

Purpose

Students measure ground-level ozone to learn how it contributes to air pollution.

Time Required

Six 45-minute class periods
Day 1: 45 minutes to discuss stratospheric and ground-level ozone
Days 2–6: 15 minutes before and after class to collect data

Lab Ratings

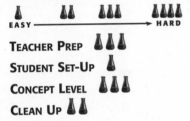

EASY ———————→ HARD

TEACHER PREP
STUDENT SET-UP
CONCEPT LEVEL
CLEAN UP

Advance Preparation

Order Eco Badge® paper test strips and colorimetric charts from a scientific supply house. Separate the test strips along the perforations, and quickly return the cards to the pouch. Reseal the pouch, removing as much air as possible to protect the test strips from moisture.

Safety Information

Students should wash their hands after handling the test strips. Approve of all test sites before allowing students to proceed with their experiments.

Teaching Strategies

This activity works best with groups of 4–5 students. Begin by helping students distinguish between stratospheric (upper atmosphere) and ground-level ozone. The following information may be helpful in your discussion: Ozone is a form of oxygen. While most oxygen molecules in our atmosphere consist of two atoms (O_2), ozone molecules are made of three oxygen atoms (O_3). Most atmospheric ozone is located in the stratosphere, which is called the *ozone layer*. Ozone molecules in the stratosphere absorb ultraviolet (UV) radiation. Depletion of ozone in the stratosphere is a serious environmental problem. Because of this absorption, the ozone layer shields the Earth from about 90 percent of the sun's UV radiation. Ground-level ozone, the primary component of smog, forms when sunlight reacts with nitrogen oxides and hydrocarbons produced by motor exhaust, gasoline vapors, and industrial emissions. Ground-level ozone is hazardous to humans, animals, and plants.

Each group should monitor different test sites and post signs requesting that others not disturb the equipment. Students can record wind data from a radio or television newscast. To help students compare data among classes, average each class's ozone readings and post the averages.

After the activity, students can graph the Eco Badge® readings against the temperature readings to relate temperature to ground-level ozone pollution levels.

HELPFUL HINT

Avoid exposing test strips to light and air. Excessive exposure can cause the test strips to fade.

Evaluation Strategies

 For help evaluating this lab, see the Checklist for Teacher Evaluation of Lesson in the *Assessment Checklists & Rubrics*. This checklist is also available in the *Classroom Management CD-ROM*.

Christopher Wood
Western Rockingham
Middle School
Madison, North Carolina

LIFE SCIENCE

Name _____ Date _____ Class _____

DISCOVERY LAB

There's Something in the Air

While playing in Dr. Eon's time machine, you transport yourself 20 years into the future. Leaving the time machine, you walk into a thick, smoggy cloud of dust. Wait a minute! Where is the clear blue sky? Why are all the people here wearing oxygen masks? This is terrible. You thought all the doomsayers were quacks. You never imagined pollution could get *this* bad.

You must warn everyone! Return to your own time and tell people about ozone pollution. Measure the ozone levels, and explain how to remedy the situation. Help save our air before it's too late!

MATERIALS
• 2 Eco Badge® filter-paper test strips
• 2 low-range plastic-backed thermometers
• transparent tape
• meterstick
• 25 cm string
• metric ruler
• small flag
• magnetic compass
• colorimetric chart

SCIENTIFIC METHOD

Ask a Question

Where are the highest levels of ground-level ozone found?

Make a Prediction

1. In your ScienceLog, list five indoor locations and five outdoor locations that may have high levels of ground-level ozone. Have your teacher approve one indoor location and one outdoor location to test ozone levels.

Conduct an Experiment

2. Get two test strips from your teacher. You will use Eco Badge® test strips to measure ground-level ozone. The strips change color in the presence of ground-level ozone.

3. Go to your selected indoor location. Tape the test strip and a thermometer about 1.5 m above the ground. Keep the test strip away from any absorptive surfaces that might react with ground-level ozone, such as paint or rubber.

Wind Speed Chart

Observation	Speed (km/h)
String, flag, and leaves do not move	0–1.6
String moves slightly	1.6–5
Feel the wind; leaves rustle	6–11
Leaves move constantly; flag straight out	12–19
Small branches move; wind lifts leaves	20–28
Small trees move	29–39
Large tree branches move	40–50
Entire trees move	51–60
Dangerous gales, storms, and hurricanes	61+

4. Repeat step 3 for the other test strip at your approved outdoor location.

5. **Measure wind speed.** Tie a piece of string to a ruler so most of the string hangs freely. Place a pile of leaves in an open outdoor area. Near the leaves, set up a small, free-standing flag. Stand near the flag and the leaf pile, and hold the ruler horizontally. Observe the movement of the string, the leaves, and the flag. Use your observations and the wind speed chart to determine the wind speed. Record the speed in your ScienceLog.

There's Something in the Air, continued

6. **Determine wind direction and cloud cover.** If the wind is too slight to move the string, wet your finger and hold it up. Face the direction that feels the coldest on your finger. Use the compass to determine which way you are facing. That is the direction of the wind. Record this direction and a cloud cover estimate in your ScienceLog.

7. **Retrieve the test strips.** After 1 hour of exposure, collect your indoor and outdoor test strips. At that time, record the temperatures at the test sites in your ScienceLog. Label the strips with the date, time, and location. Bring the test strips back to the classroom.

Collect Data

8. Compare the test strips to the colorimetric chart. Record your results in your ScienceLog in a table like the one below.

Pollution Data Table

		Temp	Wind direction	Wind speed (km/h)	Cloud cover (0–100%)	Eco Badge® reading (in ppb)	Safe/unsafe
Day 1	Indoor						
	Outdoor						
Day 2	Indoor						
	Outdoor						

9. The Environmental Protection Agency (EPA) has set the unsafe level for an hour of ground-level ozone exposure at 120 parts per billion (120 ppb). Indicate on the chart whether the ozone levels recorded were safe or unsafe.

10. Repeat steps 2–9 each day for 5 days.

Analyze the Results

11. How did wind, cloud cover, and temperature affect your ozone readings?

_____

_____

_____

LIFE SCIENCE

Analyze the Results

12. Which location had the highest measured level of ground ozone pollution?

_____

_____

_____

13. Compare your results with the results from other classes. During which part of the day was the ground-level ozone count the highest? Explain your answer.

_____

_____

_____

_____

Draw Conclusions

14. What atmospheric conditions seem to be connected with high levels of ozone pollution?

_____

_____

_____

15. What can people do to reduce ozone levels on days when ground-level ozone might be high?

_____

_____

_____

_____

10 **TEACHER'S PREPARATORY GUIDE**

DISCOVERY LAB

Rock of Ages

Purpose

Students collect and identify rock samples in order to piece together a geological history of their area.

Time Required

Two 45-minute class periods

Lab Ratings

EASY ———————→ HARD

TEACHER PREP

STUDENT SET-UP

CONCEPT LEVEL

CLEAN UP

Advance Preparation

Locate a collection site. The best place to collect rock samples is at a cliff face, especially one that was created to make way for a road. Creeks, parks, quarries, and stream beds are also good collection sites. If your school is in a city, stream beds are the best sites for rock collection. Obtain rock samples and a wall chart to help students identify their rocks. It may also be helpful to have rock and mineral field guides as references.

Safety Information

Watch for traffic and falling rocks. Make sure students stay in their groups and can see you at all times. Encourage students to wear gardening gloves while collecting rocks, and instruct students not to pick flowers or touch plants. Plants can cause skin and eye irritation. Because rock edges are sharp, students should exercise caution while handling rocks.

Teaching Strategies

This activity works best with groups of 4–5 students. Begin by pointing out to students the variety of minerals in a rock and the way the materials fit together. Ask students to list the basic characteristics used for rock identification *(composition, texture, grain size, shape, and crystal color)*.

You may wish to demonstrate how to use the identification key with a rock sample before students use the key to categorize their samples. To clarify different parts of the key, display rocks that illustrate the various characteristics. Students can then compare their samples with the rocks on display. The identification key works well for igneous and sedimentary rocks and less well for metamorphic rocks.

Metamorphism is characterized by new minerals, textures, structures, or a combination of the three. Often a rock is so changed metamorphically that it may be difficult to identify the original rock. Provide index cards so students can label their samples for display purposes. You may wish to assign a number to each of the rocks used in your classroom. Keep a record of the type of each rock and the group that examined each rock so that you can check the results.

After the activity, combine information from the students' ScienceLogs, and write it on the chalkboard. Ask students what type of rock was most predominant. As a class, discuss the area's geologic history.

Evaluation Strategies

For help evaluating this lab, see the Basic Rubric for Written Work, the Rubric for Writing Assignments, and the Checklist for Self-Evaluation of Lesson in the *Assessment Checklists & Rubrics*. These resources are also available in the *Classroom Management CD-ROM*.

EARTH SCIENCE

CLASSROOM TESTED & APPROVED

Clayton Cook
Douglas Junior High
Willis, California

10 **STUDENT WORKSHEET**

DISCOVERY LAB

Rock of Ages

The National Organization for Rocks' Rights (NORR) is tired of the treatment rocks are getting. Rocks are stepped on, kicked, thrown, bulldozed, and run over by cars. Enough is enough!

   Rocks have been on the planet a long time—longer than your parents, the trees in the forest, or your teacher. Every time you tread on a rock, you tread on our geologic history. Rocks can give us information about geologic events that took place before recorded history. If rocks could talk, what tales they would tell!

   NORR implores you to get to know your local rocks. Take one to lunch. Find out where it came from. Ask what made your rock the rock it is today. Find out the *real* story, and then tell the world how special rocks truly are.

MATERIALS

- gardening gloves
- permanent marker
- masking tape
- magnifying glass
- small bag to carry samples
- small brush to remove debris (optional)

SAFETY ALERT!

Some rocks have sharp edges. Use caution when handling them.

Objective

Collect and identify rock samples in your community to piece together a geological history of the area.

Collect Rocks

1. In your ScienceLog make a table like the one shown below. Leave plenty of space to describe the rocks. Give the table a title.

Sample number	Location found	Rock type	Characteristics	History
1				

2. In the field. Have each group member collect two rock samples. Label each rock as it is collected. In your table describe where the rock was found.

Classify Rocks

3. In class. Follow the steps in the key at right. Determine if part *a* or part *b* is true, then follow the directions. Repeat this process until you classify the rock as sedimentary (S), metamorphic (M), or igneous (I). Record the rock type in your ScienceLog.

> **Identification Key**
>
> 1. a. The rock is made of particles or of more than one material. **GO TO 2.**
>   b. Only one material can be seen. **GO TO 5.**
> 2. a. The particles fit together tightly (interlocking). **GO TO 3.**
>   b. The particles look like they are cemented together. (noninterlocking). **S**
> 3. a. There is only one kind of particle. **M**
>   b. More than one kind of particle can be seen. **GO TO 4.**
> 4. a. The particles do not form an organized pattern. **I**
>   b. The particles are lined up. **M**
> 5. a. The rock looks glassy or has many holes. **I**
>   b. The rock is made of sheetlike layers. **M**

Rock of Ages, continued

4. Repeat step 3 for the remaining rock samples.

Interpret Rock Features

5. Group the rocks according to type.

6. Examine a rock from the first group. Study the rock's appearance with a magnifying glass. Use the table for the rock's type on page 41 or 42 to find out the history of the rock. Record the characteristics and history of the sample in your ScienceLog.

7. Repeat step 6 for each rock sample.

8. In your ScienceLog, write a story about the geological history of your area. Base the story on your findings.

Sedimentary Rock (S)

As rocks are weathered, crumbled pieces of rock called *sediment* are carried by wind, water, or ice to a new area. Sedimentary rocks form as sediment deposits in layers. As time passes, the layers are buried and pressed together to form sedimentary rocks.

Characteristics	Cause	Effect
Peeling layers, like onion skins	temperature change	splits the rock and peels surface layers
Reddish with many compacted sand grains	wind	distributes sand and compacts sand into rock layers
Rounded or smooth surface; not found on a mountain	running water	smoothes the surface of the rock
Angular fragments of rock	wind	breaks a small rock from a cliff
Coarse fragments; minerals are visible	acidic rainwater	dissolves minerals and deposits them in the rock below
Coarse fragments; layered minerals	acidic rainwater	dissolves minerals from different altitudes, then redeposits them in the same place
Smooth; found on mountain	slightly melted glaciers or snow	passes over rocks and smoothes the edges
Rock is scratched; found in or near mountainous area	glaciers or snow with small rocks	passes over rocks and leaves a scratched surface
Rock has fossils and/or is porous; rock is white-gray in color	ocean water	creates porous rocks and rocks with fossils
Glassy black or gray color inside, powdery white outside; sharp edges; close circles within circles on newly exposed surface	physical and chemical changes of rocks containing silica in lakes or oceans	creates rocks with sharp edges or points
Many crystals	evaporation of sea water	leaves behind salt that crystallizes into rock
Feels sticky when wet; gray, black, white, red, or yellowish	formation in deep water	gives a smooth texture and fine grains
Glassy black fragments	lava	cools quickly and forms fragments within a rock

EARTH SCIENCE

Rock of Ages, continued

Igneous Rock (I)

Igneous rock forms when magma cools and hardens. When magma erupts as lava from a volcano, it cools quickly at the surface. Sometimes magma cools slowly below the Earth's crust, forming crystals, and comes to the surface only after the rocks above the crystals have eroded.

Characteristics	Cause	Effect
Medium or fine crystals	magma cooled beneath the Earth's crust	forms crystals; the slower the magma cools, the larger the crystals
Few crystals, very fine grains, and a somewhat glassy appearance	magma partially cooled beneath the Earth's crust	produces very few crystals
Very dark or black color with fine grains	magma cooled in water	forms no crystals; may form six-sided columns or holes from gas
Shiny and black with a glassy texture; sharp edges and closely spaced arcs where the rock has broken off	magma cooled above the Earth's crust	forms no crystals

Metamorphic Rock (M)

As tectonic plates move, high temperatures melt igneous or sedimentary rock, and high pressure folds or squeezes the rock. The heat and pressure cause minerals to recrystallize and form new minerals. Metamorphic rock also forms when magma flows into cracks and melts the surrounding rock.

Characteristics	Cause	Effect
Fine equally sized grains; contains white crystals; is easily scratched with a knife	very high temperatures	grows new crystals of calcite on limestone to form marble
Medium equally sized grains; flaky or scaly texture	high temperature	forms slate out of shale or mud
Minerals separate into bands; layers may be irregular where the rock has been folded under pressure	high temperature and pressure	changes igneous and sedimentary rocks to gneiss with coarse grains
Splits into slabs or thin plates; dark gray, shiny, flaky, or scaly texture with equally sized grains	high pressure	during mountain formation, squeezes shale and forms slate

Whether It Weathers (or Not)

Purpose

Students simulate the weathering of rocks to investigate how water, ice, and air pollutants affect the rate of weathering.

Time Required

Two 45-minute class periods

Lab Ratings

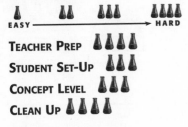

EASY → HARD

TEACHER PREP ▲▲▲▲
STUDENT SET-UP ▲▲▲
CONCEPT LEVEL ▲▲▲
CLEAN UP ▲▲▲▲

Advance Preparation

One week before the activity, ask students to bring in empty coffee cans with lids. Obtain limestone and concrete from a large garden-supply store or a home-and-builder's warehouse. Marble chips from these stores are impure and will not produce the desired results. Some local monument carvers may provide marble and granite chips at no charge. Pieces of rock should be no bigger than the size of your fist.

Limestone quality varies, and some samples may not yield good results. Conduct the experiment with a limestone sample at least a day before you plan to do the activity. You may reuse rocks in subsequent classes. Make sure a freezer is available, and clear enough space to accommodate a tray of rock samples for each group. If there is not enough freezer space available, you may wish to conduct this activity when outside temperatures reach freezing or have student volunteers conduct this portion of the activity as homework. Do not soak rocks in a sink because the rock fragments can clog the drain.

Safety Information

Vinegar is a weak acid and can irritate the skin and eyes. Students should wear safety goggles, latex gloves, and an apron.

Teaching Strategies

This activity works best with groups of 3–4 students. Before the activity, review the differences between physical and chemical weathering. Point out that these processes affect natural as well as human-made structures.

Show students where to freeze their rocks. For more dramatic results, have students refreeze and rethaw the rock samples.

Discuss how acid rain affects weathering. Rain is naturally acidic. Vinegar and water are both solvents—they dissolve substances. Vinegar is more acidic than rain, and this activity uses undiluted vinegar to produce quicker and more dramatic results. Encourage students to listen to the reaction as it takes place. Ask students to consider where the missing rock mass went.

Waste disposal: Rock fragments can clog the drain and should not be poured into the sink. The contents of the coffee can and water bucket can be used to replenish lawn or garden soil.

Evaluation Strategies

For help evaluating this lab, see the Rubric for Experiments and the Checklist for Self-Evaluation of Lesson in the *Assessment Checklists & Rubrics*. These resources are also available in the *Classroom Management CD-ROM*.

CLASSROOM TESTED & APPROVED

Steven Ramig
West Point Junior–Senior High
West Point, Nebraska

▲ EARTH SCIENCE

EcoLab

11 **STUDENT WORKSHEET**

DISCOVERY LAB

Whether It Weathers (or Not)

It is the centennial of Rain Falls, New Hampshire, where the precipitation averages 111 cm a year and the temperatures range from −11°C in the winter to 33°C in the summer. In celebration of the centennial, the town council has voted to erect a new monument in the town square.

The council has asked you to select the most durable design and material for the new monument. Two designs have been submitted for your review. One is a very detailed statue of Claude Rain, the town's founder, and the other is a simple obelisk.

Several materials have been suggested, including marble, granite, limestone, and concrete. Compare the effects of weathering on each material and design. Then submit your recommendations to the town council.

MATERIALS

- tray
- masking tape
- 2 large pieces of each of the following: granite, marble, limestone, concrete
- 150 g of each of the following: marble chips, granite chips, limestone chips, concrete chips
- magnifying glass
- bucket of water
- freezer
- 4 coffee cans with lids
- metric balance
- towel
- 500 mL beakers (4)
- graduated cylinder
- protective gloves
- 600 mL of vinegar

SCIENTIFIC **METHOD**

Ask a Question

Which monument material and design will best withstand the severe weather in Rain Falls?

Make a Prediction

1. Based on your own experience, which material do you expect to be best suited for the statue? Explain.

_____

_____

Conduct an Experiment—Part 1: Testing Materials

Investigate each environmental factor that will affect the weathering of the monument, and determine the best choice of material for your statue.

The Effects of Freezing and Thawing

2. Rain Falls has a cold, wet climate. Because the town often freezes in winter and thaws in spring, you must find out how freezing and thawing affect the rocks.

3. **Day 1:** Examine a sample of each material with a magnifying glass. Can you find any cracks where water might enter?

4. Soak each rock sample in a bucket of water for 5 minutes. Remove the samples, and place them on the tray. Do not dry the samples. Place the tray in the freezer.

5. **Day 2:** Remove the tray from the freezer, and allow the rocks to warm to room temperature.

6. Examine the samples closely. Look for any changes with a magnifying glass. In the table on page 46, describe any changes to your samples.

The Effects of Weathering by Humans

Because the monument will sit in a public area, it will be exposed to vandals and children and wear from periodic cleaning. Test how the rocks on your list will resist the forces of human weathering.

7. Place 100 g of each type of rock chip in a separate can. Add water to each container until it is half full. Place the lids on the cans. Securely tape the lids to seal the cans.

8. Steadily shake the containers for 10 minutes.

9. Open one container. Drain the water, and dry the rocks with a towel. Place the dried rocks on a balance. Measure and record the final mass in the table on page 46.

10. Repeat step 9 for the other three containers.

The Effects of Acid Rain

Because snow and rain are slightly acidic, you must test the effects of acidic precipitation on different materials.

11. Place a few small pieces of marble on a balance. Measure the initial mass, and record it in the table page 46. Place the small pieces of marble in an empty beaker.

12. Repeat step 11 for each material, putting each type of material in a separate beaker.

13. Pour 50 mL of vinegar into each beaker of rocks. Observe and listen to the reactions in all four beakers. After 10 minutes, dispose of the vinegar as directed by your teacher.

14. Dry the marble rocks with a towel. Measure the final mass of the small rocks, and record the results in the table on page 46. Calculate and record the percentage of rock lost. Record this value in the table on page 46.

15. Repeat step 14 for each of the other materials.

Part 2: Testing Designs

Keep in mind that the monument should last 100 years. The building material affects the monument's rate of weathering. Certain designs may weather differently because of the surface details. Now examine the relationship between exposed surface area and weathering.

SAFETY ALERT!

Vinegar is a weak acid. Wear safety goggles, latex gloves, and an apron while using vinegar.

EARTH SCIENCE

16. Place a large piece of marble on a balance. Measure the initial mass, and record it in the table below. Place the marble in an empty beaker.

17. Repeat step 16 for the other materials, putting each rock into a different beaker.

18. Pour 50 mL of vinegar into each beaker. Observe and listen to the reaction. After 10 minutes, dispose of the vinegar as directed by your teacher.

19. Dry the rocks with a towel. Measure the final mass of each rock, and record the results in your ScienceLog. Calculate and record the percentage of rock lost, and record this value in the table below.

HELPFUL HINT

Do not pour the samples down the drain when you are finished. Ask your teacher for the proper method of disposal.

Analyze the Results

20. Overall, which rock best resisted weathering? Explain.

_____

_____

_____

Rock Weathering Results

Rock	Marble	Granite	Limestone	Concrete
Effect of freezing and thawing the rock				
Initial mass of rock before shaking (g)	100 g	100 g	100 g	100 g
Final mass of rock after shaking (g)				
Percentage of mass lost				
Initial mass of small rocks before vinegar (g)				
Initial mass of small rocks after vinegar (g)				
Percentage of mass lost				
Initial mass of large rocks before vinegar (g)				
Initial mass of large rocks after vinegar (g)				
Percentage of mass lost				

21. Compare the percentages of mass lost for the rock types. Was the rate of chemical weathering faster on larger or smaller rocks?

_____

_____

_____

_____

22. How did the amount of exposed surface area affect the rate of weathering?

_____

_____

_____

23. Which design has more surface area, the statue or the obelisk? Explain your answer.

_____

_____

_____

Draw Conclusions

24. Justify your choice of material and design.

_____

_____

_____

_____

_____

Going Further

Carved into the face of Mount Rushmore are giant sculptures of four American presidents. Find out how scientists are using new technology to preserve Mount Rushmore.

EARTH SCIENCE

The Frogs Are Off Course

Purpose

Students test water samples to determine the effects of fertilizer runoff on a naturally occurring body of water.

Time Required

Three 45-minute class periods

Lab Ratings

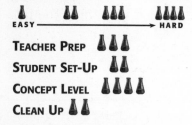

EASY ⟶ HARD

TEACHER PREP 🧪🧪🧪
STUDENT SET-UP 🧪🧪
CONCEPT LEVEL 🧪🧪🧪🧪
CLEAN UP 🧪🧪

Advance Preparation

Locate a nearby golf course with a stream. The ideal course has a stream running into and out of it. If a golf course with a stream is unavailable, find a park or well-manicured lawn with a pond or stream. Make arrangements with the golf course director or lawn owner for a class visit. Explain that your class will be conducting tests on water samples.

Obtain test kits from a local pet store (used for testing water aquariums) or a scientific supply house. A good kit will tell you the chemicals' identity and concentration. It costs less to buy the chemicals and make your own refills by reusing the original squirt bottles. Fill a 1 L plastic jug with plant food prepared according to the manufacturer's directions. Try to use a colorless fertilizer, such as Osmicote™. Dyes interfere with test results. Read the test kit instructions to familiarize yourself with the testing techniques. Results will vary with different test kits and water sources. The day before the activity, test your samples and make up a key from your results.

Safety Information

Use plastic jars, if available. If glass jars are used, discard any that show signs of chipping or cracking. Many of the chemicals in the kit are hazardous and carry warnings on the labels. Do not allow students to mix the chemicals from different kits. After each test, flush the tested water down the sink with a lot of running water. Do not use a bucket to collect the samples.

Teaching Strategies

Have students work in groups of 2–4. Review how to test the pH of a liquid. Explain that nutrients are essential to life in a stream but that when fertilizers run off into the water, the increased nutrient levels can cause algae to grow rapidly. The algae use oxygen to respire at night; when they die, their decomposition requires oxygen. This, in turn, causes the levels of dissolved oxygen in the water to decrease. Therefore, evidence of fertilizer runoff can be determined by levels of dissolved oxygen in the water.

Ask students how lawns are kept green. Explain that plants need soil that is high in nitrogen, phosphorus, and potassium. Show students the N-P-K ratings on the plant food package. Explain that these are ratios of nutrients. When soil doesn't contain the necessary concentrations of nutrients, fertilizer is used to meet the needs of the plants. Often, more fertilizer is applied than can be absorbed by the plants. Rain washes the excess fertilizer into nearby bodies of water.

Before going to the collection site, demonstrate the proper use of each test kit.

Evaluation Strategies

For help evaluating this lab, see the Checklist for Self-Evaluation of Lesson in the *Assessment Checklists & Rubrics* (also available in the *Classroom Management CD-ROM*).

CLASSROOM TESTED & APPROVED

Kenneth Creese
White Mountain Junior High
Rock Springs, Wyoming

FIELD ACTIVITY

12 **STUDENT WORKSHEET**

DISCOVERY LAB

The Frogs Are Off Course

Extra! Extra! Trumpet County Frog Numbers Are Dwindling!

The Trumpet County frog is vanishing. The Trumpet County Country Club is renowned for the twilight serenade of its amphibian inhabitants. Their sunset songs attract thousands of people to the club each year. A few years ago, there were hundreds of frogs, but now the club is silent. Where did the frogs go?

City officials believe that the golf courses have been over-fertilized and that runoff is hurting the ecosystem the frogs need in order to reproduce. Country Club management denies any overfertilization.

Instead, they believe that the frogs have gone south this year due to the dismal weather. They are sure the frogs will return in great numbers, all tanned and relaxed, when fall arrives.

City officials want you to investigate whether the Trumpet County frogs are dying or whether they are catching some rays on the beach. You will need to test the water going into and out of the golf course. While on the golf course, be careful not to get hit by a stray ball!

MATERIALS

- 5 clean jars with lids
- masking tape
- permanent marker
- 100 mL of distilled water
- 100 mL of tap water
- 100 mL of water containing plant food
- one of each of the following test kits: phosphate, pH, nitrite/nitrate, ammonia, and dissolved oxygen

SAFETY ALERT

Many chemicals in the test kits are hazardous. Read and follow the safety warnings on the labels. After each test, flush the tested water down the sink with a lot of running water.

SCIENTIFIC METHOD

Ask a Question

Does water runoff on the golf course's well-manicured lawn contain fertilizer?

Make a Prediction

1. Do you think you will find evidence of fertilizer in the water?

   _____

   _____

Conduct an Experiment

2. **In class:** Label and fill jars 1–3 as indicated in the table on page 50.

3. Perform all five water-quality tests on the contents of jars 1–3 by following the instructions accompanying the test kits. Record your results in the table on page 50.

EARTH SCIENCE

The Frogs Are Off Course, continued

---

4. **At the collection sites:** Where the stream enters the golf course, label and fill jar 4 with water. Where the stream exits the golf course, label and fill jar 5 with water.

5. **In class:** Conduct each of the five water-quality tests on each sample. Record the results in the table below.

Test Kit Results

Jar	Contents	Phosphate	Nitrite/nitrate	Ammonia	pH	Amount of dissolved oxygen
1	Distilled water					
2	Tap water					
3	Tap water with plant food					
4	Water entering					
5	Water exiting					

Analyze the Results

6. Were the nutrient levels of the water entering the golf course the same as those of the water leaving it?

_____

_____

_____

_____

_____

7. Were there traces of nutrients in the water entering the golf course? Explain your answer.

_____

_____

_____

_____

_____

The Frogs Are Off Course, continued

8. Were any of the test results different from what you expected? If so, which were different and how might you explain these differences?

_____

_____

_____

_____

_____

Draw Conclusions

9. Which explanation of the frogs' disappearance is supported by your tests? Explain your answer.

_____

_____

_____

_____

Critical Thinking

10. How might a country club maintain a green turf while decreasing the amount of polluted runoff?

_____

_____

_____

_____

11. Frogs are just one organism affected by the runoff. What other organisms could be affected?

_____

_____

_____

_____

_____

_____

EARTH SCIENCE

Operation Oil-Spill Cleanup

> ### Cooperative Learning Activity
>
> **Group size:** 4–6 students
>
> **Group goal:** Use a variety of methods to clean up a model oil spill to learn about the complexity of managing environmental emergencies.
>
> **Positive interdependence:** Each group member should choose a role, such as research coordinator, discussion leader, recorder, or materials coordinator.
>
> **Individual accountability:** After the contest, each group member should be able to discuss what worked and what didn't work during the design and performance stages of this project.

Time Required

Three 45-minute class periods: two classes to design and test the plan and one class to hold the oil-spill contest

Lab Ratings

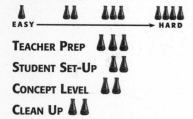

Advance Preparation

Purchase materials from a craft store, a garden supply store, or a building supply store. Cut the fake fur into 2.5 × 8 cm strips. Adding food coloring to the water will make the oil more visible. To make the model more realistic, use a 3.5% saltwater solution (made by adding 35 g of salt to 965 mL of water) in place of tap water.

Safety Information

Feathers collected from the field may contain pathogens. If such feathers are used, instruct students to keep the feathers away from their face and have them wash their hands following the activity.

Teaching Strategies

Begin by asking students what they know about major oil spills. You might have them read a magazine article about an actual oil spill and its cleanup, such as

"A Clot in the Heart of the Earth," *Outside,* June 1989, about the 1989 *Exxon Valdez* oil spill. Students may be surprised to learn of the sophisticated methods used to clean up spills. Offshore oil drills and oil supertankers, particularly those with single hulls, can cause oil spills that damage fishing grounds, spoil beaches, kill marine birds and mammals, and destroy shellfish beds. Some animals suffocate when oil covers their breathing apparatus; some animals ingest oil, which may be toxic to them; and some, such as furred and feathered animals, have their means of insulation damaged.

You may wish to specify a time interval (such as 5 minutes) within which the cleanup should be completed. One liter of oil can contaminate up to 5 million liters of water.

Encourage students to do library research about oil-spill cleanup methods.

Evaluation Strategies

For help evaluating this lab, see the Checklist for Teacher Evaluation of Lesson and the Checklist for Group Evaluation of Cooperative Group Activity in the *Assessment Checklists & Rubrics.* These checklists are also available in the *Classroom Management CD-ROM.*

Steven Ramig
West Point Junior–Senior High
West Point, Nebraska

Name _____ Date _____ Class _____

DISCOVERY LAB

Operation Oil-Spill Cleanup

To: All Eco-Marine staff
From: Marina Waters, President
Subject: Oil-Spill Cleanup Proposal

Megacrude Oil Company is accepting contract proposals for an emergency cleanup plan. The plan would be followed if an oil spill is caused by a Megacrude supertanker. Several top-notch companies are competing for this contract. We need to show Megacrude that Eco-Marine can do the best job. We must develop a plan for a cleanup that is fast, effective, and minimally harmful to the environment.

Each work team will develop its own plan. First test cleanup materials. Then develop a comprehensive cleanup plan. We will then test all plans and submit the best plan to Megacrude. Good luck!

Marina Waters

MATERIALS

- cleanup supplies: brown paper bags, craft sticks, detergent, dip nets, drinking straws, spoons, toothpicks, plastic wrap, string, aluminum foil, cloth, cotton balls, nylon stockings, paper towels, plastic foam, coffee filters, sawdust, and wood shavings
- 3 shallow pans
- water
- 100 mL of cooking oil
- 5 mL spoon
- pebbles
- sand or gravel
- 2.5 × 8 cm strips of fake fur
- feathers
- 50 mL beaker
- latex gloves
- watch or clock that indicates seconds

SCIENTIFIC METHOD

Ask a Question

What is the best method for cleaning up a model oil spill?

Form a Hypothesis

1. From the materials list, select 5–10 supplies that you think would best clean up an oil spill. Of the supplies you selected, which one do you think will work best? Write your hypothesis in your ScienceLog.

Test the Hypothesis

2. Add 0.5 L of water to a shallow pan. Pour 5 mL of oil onto the surface of the water to model an oil spill on the open ocean.

3. In another container, make a model of a shoreline by adding rocks, sand, gravel, fake fur, and feathers. Let the fake fur represent sea mammals and the feathers represent birds. Pour a small amount of oil onto your model.

4. Make a table in your ScienceLog like the one on page 54. Test the effectiveness of the supplies for each category. Based on the results of these preliminary tests, rate each material as poor, average, good, or excellent.

EARTH SCIENCE

Evaluation of Cleaning Supplies

Cleaning material	Oil-spill containment	Water cleanup & oil recovery	Shore cleanup	Wildlife cleanup	Environmental impact

Draw Conclusions

5. As a team, decide which materials were most effective at cleaning up the oil. Determine which materials and techniques your team will use for each of the following:
- oil-spill containment
- water cleanup and oil recovery
- cleanup of shore and wildlife
- minimization of the impact of your cleanup operations on the ocean ecosystem

6. Devise a plan. Summarize the important components of each idea you came up with in step 5. Based on your discussion, develop a plan in your ScienceLog for how your team can best accomplish the cleanup. Write detailed instructions for cleaning up an oil spill with the supplies you tested.

7. Build a model. Build a model ocean in a pan. Create a shore using sand, gravel, and a few rocks at one end of the pan. Place a feather and a fur strip at the shoreline.

8. Carefully add 0.5 L of water. Let a small beaker of oil represent your supertanker. Spill 50 mL of oil into the center of your water area. Gently blow the oil toward the shore.

9. Test your plan. Check the time, and implement the cleanup plan as quickly as possible. For each cleanup task listed in step 5 (oil-spill containment, oil recovery, shore cleanup, and wildlife cleanup), record how long it takes to complete the task and how well the cleanup works in your ScienceLog.

> **HELPFUL HINT**
>
> Protect your clothing from oil by wearing an apron during the oil-spill cleanup.

Analyze Results

10. Was it possible to recover any of the oil? Could the recovery method that worked best be used in a real oil spill?

_____

_____

_____

Operation Oil-Spill Cleanup, continued

---

11. What happened when the oil reached the beach? How effective was the cleanup of sand and wildlife?

_____

_____

_____

_____

_____

12. What factors might make a real cleanup different from your simulation?

_____

_____

_____

_____

_____

Communicate Results

13. After all teams have finished their cleanup, present your results to the class. Vote to determine which plan should be submitted to Megacrude Oil Company.

14. Which cleanup plan worked best? Explain your answer.

_____

_____

_____

Critical Thinking

15. In a real oil spill, how might cleanup methods affect animal life?

_____

_____

_____

_____

EARTH SCIENCE

14 TEACHER'S PREPARATORY GUIDE

MAKING MODELS

That Greenhouse Effect!

Purpose

Students model different surface conditions in order to learn about the greenhouse effect.

Time Required

Two 45-minute class periods

Lab Ratings

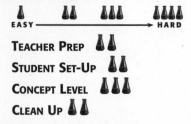

EASY ———————————→ HARD

TEACHER PREP 🍶🍶

STUDENT SET-UP 🍶🍶

CONCEPT LEVEL 🍶🍶🍶

CLEAN UP 🍶🍶

Advance Preparation

One week before the activity, have students each bring in a pair of identical large glass jars. Designate a bright, sunny spot for the experiment. Although a grassy area creates a closer simulation of Earth's conditions, a concrete or asphalt area yields more-dramatic results.

Safety Information

Discard any glass jars that show signs of chipping or cracking. Use alcohol thermometers instead of mercury thermometers to minimize the risk to students in case of breakage. Use nontoxic paint, such as latex or water-based paint.

Teaching Strategies

This activity works best in groups of 2–3 students. Divide the class into five groups, and have each group test different conditions. Ask students if they have ever entered a car on a cold but sunny day to discover that the car's interior was warmer than the outside air. Solar energy passed through the glass windows and raised the temperature of the car's interior. Thermal energy does not pass as easily through the glass and was therefore trapped inside the car. Point out that this is an example of the greenhouse effect. Ask students what they have heard about the greenhouse effect.

Have students shield their thermometer bulbs from the sun to avoid inaccurately high readings. The jar covered with plastic wrap should be warmer than the open jar. Students should find that light-colored surfaces are cooler than dark-colored surfaces because sunlight is reflected from light-colored surfaces and absorbed by dark-colored surfaces. Air over dry soil should be warmer than air over wet soil. Air over land should be warmer than air over water (although in the winter, air over oceans can be warmer than air over land). Plants should keep the air temperature cooler. Air over ice should heat more slowly than air of a moderate temperature. Have students compare results with others in the class.

Evaluation Strategies

For help evaluating this lab, see the Rubric for Performance Assessment and the Checklist for Teacher Evaluation of Lesson in the *Assessment Checklists & Rubrics*. These resources are also available in the *Classroom Management CD-ROM*.

Clayton Cook
Douglas Junior High
Willis, California

FIELD ACTIVITY

14 STUDENT WORKSHEET

MAKING MODELS

That Greenhouse Effect!

Welcome to another round of *That Greenhouse Effect!*—the game show on which the contestants not only predict outcomes but also use their keen intellect while working against the clock. I am your host Blaise Haht. Today, contestants are warming up to investigate the results of the greenhouse effect. First let's introduce the contestants.

Meet Professor Luke Wharm, who will determine whether the air above light surfaces or the air above dark surfaces is cooler. At the water-versus-land station is Ms. Sylvia Aguapher, two-time medalist in swimming. Mr. Phil Ruetrot, a landscape architect, is at the wet-soil-versus-dry-soil station. Mr. Ed Blooms, a local paleobotanist, will be at the plants-versus-no-plants station. And last but not least, Ms. Lilith Friese, a professional ice-wall climber, will test the effects of ice and snow on the greenhouse effect.

Each contestant will have 40 minutes to construct two greenhouse models and determine which condition is cooler. Let's get the game going. Grab a jar, and check out the heat!

MATERIALS

- 2 index cards
- transparent tape
- 2 thermometers
- 2 large glass jars of the same size and shape
- clear plastic wrap
- 2 rubber bands
- watch or clock
- one or more of the following items: black and white latex paint, water, soil, sod, plants, ice cubes
- straightedge or ruler
- graph paper

SCIENTIFIC METHOD

Ask a Question

How do different surface conditions contribute to the temperature of Earth's atmosphere?

Make a Prediction: Round 1

1. In the first round, you have 20 minutes to construct a model and determine what would happen if sunlight were trapped in Earth's atmosphere. Write your prediction in your ScienceLog.

Conduct an Experiment

2. **Inside:** Tape an index card around the bulb of each thermometer to shield the bulb from the sun.

3. Tape each thermometer inside a jar so that the bulb doesn't touch the bottom of the jar, as shown at right.

4. In your ScienceLog, draw a table like the one on page 58. In your data table, record the initial temperature of both thermometers.

5. Cover the opening of one jar with plastic wrap. Secure the wrap with a rubber band. This jar will model the greenhouse effect on Earth while the uncovered jar serves as a control.

6. **Outside:** Place the jars in a bright, sunny spot. Read both thermometers every 2 minutes for 10 minutes. Record the temperatures in your data table.

▲ EARTH SCIENCE

Greenhouse-Model Temperature Data

Observation point	Temperature (°C) control jar	Temperature (°C) experimental jar
Initial temperature in the sun		
2 min		
4 min		
6 min		
8 min		
10 min		

Form a Hypothesis: Round 2

7. Many scientists believe that the Earth's surface will heat up as greenhouse gases build up in the atmosphere. But they don't expect all parts of the Earth to warm equally. Consider the following questions:

- Which will heat faster, the air over snow-covered plains or the air over newly plowed fields?
- Which will heat faster, air over the ocean or air over land?
- Does vegetation affect the rate of global warming?
- How does the amount of moisture in the soil affect the rate of global warming?
- Does the temperature of the land affect the temperature of the air above it?

Generate a hypothesis based on one of the questions, and record the hypothesis in your ScienceLog.

Make a Prediction

8. Design an experiment that will test your hypothesis. Reuse the jars you used in steps 1–6. Sketch your design in your ScienceLog.

9. Based on your experimental design in step 8, predict the results that you expect. Write your prediction below.

_____

_____

_____

_____

_____

Test the Hypothesis

10. Test your hypothesis. Create a data table in your ScienceLog similar to the one you made before. Describe the conditions of each jar listed in the column headings. Be sure to cover both jars with plastic wrap. Record the results of your experiment in the table. Graph your data. Note any changes you made to your experiment.

Analyze the Results

11. Was your prediction correct? Explain.

_____

_____

_____

12. How did the experiment model the variation in warming in different parts of the world?

_____

_____

_____

_____

13. How does your model differ from the real "greenhouse Earth?"

_____

_____

_____

_____

_____

_____

_____

_____

EARTH SCIENCE

DISCOVERY LAB

Rain Maker or Rain Faker?

Purpose

Students make observations and record data from weather instruments in order to learn to predict weather patterns.

Time Required

One 45-minute class period and 20 minutes daily for 1 week to observe, record, and discuss the daily findings

Lab Ratings

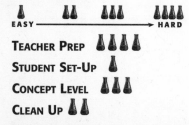

EASY ———————→ HARD

TEACHER PREP

STUDENT SET-UP

CONCEPT LEVEL

CLEAN UP

ADDITIONAL MATERIALS

- barometer
- anemometer
- sling psychrometer (optional)
For psychrometer
- empty 1.9 L milk carton
- scissors
- 15 cm shoelace
- 2 low-range, plastic-backed alcohol thermometers
- twist-tie
- 2 rubber bands
- water
- plastic wrap
- transparent tape
For rain gauge
- small jar
- metric ruler
- permanent marker

Advance Preparation

Conduct this activity in the fall or spring. Obtain the additional materials from a craft store and a scientific supply house. If an anemometer is too expensive or is unavailable, you can find directions for making one by searching for "anemometer" on the Internet. Find an open area to set up a weather station where the instruments

won't be disturbed by humans, direct wind, or direct sun. Trees should not obstruct the rain gauge. You may wish to contact your local weather station to invite a meteorologist to class. Some weather stations sponsor schools, lending equipment and assistance free of charge.

All classes can use the same weather station. *Weather Proverbs,* by George Frier, Ph.D., lists more weather sayings. For additional information, contact the education office of the National Weather Bureau.

Make a psychrometer. Cut the top from the milk carton. Poke a hole 5 cm from the bottom of the milk carton. Slide the shoelace over a thermometer's bulb, and secure it in place with a twist tie. Use rubber bands to affix the thermometers to the outside of the carton, on the same side of the carton as the hole. Pull the loose end of the shoelace through the hole. Pour water 3 cm deep into the carton. Cover the

Milk carton (top removed)

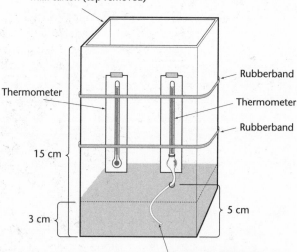

Thermometer

Rubberband

Thermometer

Rubberband

15 cm

3 cm

5 cm

Shoelace

continued...

CLASSROOM
TESTED & APPROVED

Steven Ramig
West Point Junior–Senior High
West Point, Nebraska

carton's opening with plastic wrap to minimize evaporation. Add water daily to compensate for evaporation, or use a sling psychrometer to measure relative humidity. **Make a rain gauge.** Hold a ruler against a jar so that the 0 cm mark is at the bottom. Starting at the bottom of the jar, mark 0.5 cm increments along the side of the jar.

Safety Information

Students should use alcohol thermometers instead of mercury thermometers. Mercury is extremely poisonous. Students should not attempt to measure winds above 61 km/h.

Teaching Strategies

This activity works best in groups of 2–4 students. Begin the activity by asking students how meteorologists forecast the weather. Discuss how observations of cloud types and movement and the measurement of factors such as temperature, humidity, and wind speed are used as data to predict—or forecast—the weather. Meteorologists now have sophisticated equipment to measure and model weather conditions, but in the past they had to rely on simple equipment and shared knowledge, such as that in proverbs.

Ask students to help you list weather proverbs on the board. Tell students they will use some of these proverbs to forecast the weather. Scientific explanations for proverbs in this activity are as follows:

Red sky: Most weather patterns in North America move from west to east. If the sky is red in the evening, the western sky is usually clear, indicating no incoming storm. If the sky is red in the morning, it means the western sky has clouds reflecting the sunlight, and a storm may be brewing.

Swallows: High air pressure, which produces fair weather, creates currents that lift flying insects higher into the atmosphere, causing hungry swallows to follow. Low air pressure, which precedes a storm, drives the insects and swallows closer to the ground.

Clouds: Low clouds signal the possibility of rain.

Dew: On cool, clear nights, moisture condenses on plants to form dew.

You may wish to familiarize students with compound names of clouds. Cumulo nimbus and nimbo stratus, for example, are two types of rain clouds.

Each day a representative from each group should collect weather data and share the information with his or her group. After your last class, empty the contents of the rain gauge. If it rains over the course of the school day, give the data read by the last class to the earlier classes. Spend 10–15 minutes at the end of the week reviewing and discussing the week's data. You may need to ask leading questions each day until students observe patterns and make connections.

Generally, if the barometric pressure is falling or if thunderclouds appear, one can expect rain. High, steady pressure or rising pressure are associated with fair weather. When temperatures drop and clouds dissipate, expect clear skies.

Evaluation Strategies

For help evaluating this lab, see the Rubric for Performance Assessment and the Rubric for Writing Assignment in the *Assessment Checklists & Rubrics*. These rubrics are also available in the *Classroom Management CD-ROM*.

EARTH SCIENCE

FIELD ACTIVITY

15 STUDENT WORKSHEET

DISCOVERY LAB

Rain Maker or Rain Faker?

Snake-Oil Magee is coming back to swindle the good farmers of Nigh Eve. He claims to have a secret rain-making formula that's guaranteed to pull the rain right out of the sky! This morning as the sun rose into a red sky, Magee poured some of his formula onto the ground. Within a few hours it started raining!

The farmers want the formula. Last year was a drought year, and this year may not be any different. The farmers are ready to pay anything to save their crops and their farms. Magee is already counting his money.

Fortunately, you are weather wise. You know that Magee's secret is in his weather savvy, not his formula, and you remember an old saying about a red sky meaning rain. Magee is staying for only 1 week. You've got that long to uncover his real secret before the farmers give him all of their money and Magee is gone with the wind.

MATERIALS

- 20 cm of string
- ruler
- scissors
- directional compass

USEFUL TERMS

barometer
device used to measure atmospheric pressure

anemometer
device used to measure wind speed

psychrometer
device used to determine relative humidity

relative humidity
the percentage of water in the air relative to the maximum amount the air can hold at a given temperature

SCIENTIFIC
METHOD

Ask a Question

Which weather observations, measurements, or proverbs are most helpful in predicting weather?

Form a Hypothesis

1. Before people had instruments to measure weather, they made a lot of observations. They learned that nature gives clues about the upcoming weather. To remember the meaning of the clues, people created catchy sayings. Many people still use the proverbs below.
   - Red sky at morning, sailors take warning; red sky at night, sailor's delight.
   - Fair weather's nigh if swallows fly high; a storm will blow if swallows fly low.
   - When clouds look like rocks and towers, Earth will be refreshed by showers.
   - Rain will not pass if there's dew on the grass.

2. Pick two other weather proverbs from the list created by your class, and write them in your ScienceLog.

3. Do you think these proverbs are true predictors of weather? Write your hypothesis in your ScienceLog.

Procedure

4. **Prepare a data table.** For the next week, you will observe and record weather data. Make a table in your ScienceLog like the one on page 63.

Weather Data

	Day 1	Day 2
Types of clouds observed		
Observations		
Weather proverb(s)		
Estimated wind speed (km/h)		
Estimated wind direction		
Observation-based prediction		
Temperature (°C)		
Pressure (mm-Hg)		
Measured wind speed (km/h)		
Relative humidity (%)		
Measurement-based prediction		
Rain level (cm)		
Observed weather		

5. **Get to know the clouds.** Review the cloud terms below. Use the cloud names to describe the cloud types in your ScienceLog. You may combine the cloud names to make up compound names.

Meanings of Cloud Names

Name	Meaning	Description
Cirrus	curl	thin, wispy, made of ice ("mares' tails")
Stratus	layer or blanket	sheetlike, resembles lifted fog
Cumulus	heap	looks like cotton puffs or sheep
Nimbus	rain	thick, dark, can be patchy

Make Observations

Each day, complete the observations and data collection in steps 6–11 and record the information in the data table in your ScienceLog.

6. **Observe the clouds.** Every morning, observe the cloud formations. Draw the clouds. Use the terms in the charts above to help you identify and record the cloud types.

7. **Choose a weather proverb.** Review the list of weather proverbs on page 62. Did any describe today's weather? Record the proverb.

EARTH SCIENCE

Estimating Wind Speed (km/h)

Observation	Speed
String, leaves, and flag don't move	0–1
Flag waves, string and leaves move	1–19
Branches and small trees sway	20–38
Large branches and large trees move	38–61

8. Estimate the wind speed. On your way to school, did you notice the wind on your face or see leaves constantly moving along the sidewalk? Did the trees sway? If the wind seems rather still, tie a piece of string to a ruler so that it can swing freely, and observe its movement. Use the chart at left to determine the wind speed. Record the estimated speed.

9. Determine the wind direction. Face the wind. If the wind is too slight to feel, wet your finger, hold it up to the wind, and face the direction that feels coldest. Use the compass to determine which way you are facing. Record this direction.

Make a Prediction—Observation-Based

10. What will the weather be? Based on your selected proverb and recorded data, record your weather prediction in the first prediction row of your chart.

Collect Data

11. Measure the relative humidity. On the psychrometer, read the temperature on the wet-bulb thermometer. Subtract the wet-bulb temperature from the dry-bulb temperature. Use the chart below to find the percentage of relative humidity. Record this value.

Measuring the Moisture (Relative Humidity*)

Dry-bulb minus wet bulb (°C)	Dry-bulb temperature (°C)							
	−1°	5°	10°	15°	21°	26°	32°	37°
0.5	90	92	93	94	95	96	96	97
1.1	79	84	87	89	90	92	92	93
1.6	68	76	80	84	86	87	88	90
2.2	58	68	74	78	81	83	85	86
3.3	38	52	61	68	72	75	78	80
4.4	18	67	49	58	64	68	71	74
5.5		22	37	48	55	61	65	68
6.6		8	26	39	48	54	59	62
7.7			16	30	40	47	53	57
8.8			5	21	33	41	47	51
9.9				13	26	35	41	47
11.0				5	19	29	36	42
12.1					12	23	32	37
13.2					6	18	26	33

*Relative-humidity values are expressed as percentages.

---

12. **Measure the temperature** using the dry-bulb thermometer. Record your data in your ScienceLog.

13. **Measure the atmospheric pressure** using the barometer. Record your data in your ScienceLog.

14. **Measure the wind speed** using the anemometer, if available. Record your data in your ScienceLog.

15. **Measure the rainfall** using the rain gauge. Without disturbing the jar, read the mark that is aligned with the water level. Record your data in your ScienceLog.

Make a Prediction—Measurement-Based

16. Predict the weather based on your measurements in the second prediction row of your chart.

Analyze the Results

You made predictions using different types of information. One type was based on weather proverbs and observations, and the other type was based on measurements from instruments. Answer the questions below in your ScienceLog.

17. **At home:** Observe the weather when you're not at school, and record your observations. Compare your two predictions. Was either prediction correct? Was one more reliable than the other?

_____

_____

_____

18. Did the proverbs help you to predict the weather? Give an example.

_____

_____

_____

Draw Conclusions

19. Write a one-page paper persuading farmers to predict weather on their own. How would you tell the farmers of Nigh Eve to forecast the weather using only observations (no instruments). Explain which instruments they might find most useful in making accurate predictions.

▲ **EARTH SCIENCE**

There's a Space for Us

Cooperative Learning Activity

Group size: 4–8 students

Group goal: Students design a self-sustaining colony on Mars to understand how humans use their environment wisely.

Positive interdependence: Each group member should choose and develop one of the following components: water, air, electricity, or food.

Individual accountability: After the activity, each team member should be able to explain how the colony functions and the logic in the group's design.

Time Required

Three 45-minute class periods. A suggested pacing guide is provided on page 67.

Lab Ratings

🧪   🧪🧪   🧪🧪🧪   🧪🧪🧪🧪
EASY ⟶ HARD

TEACHER PREP 🧪

STUDENT SET-UP 🧪

CONCEPT LEVEL 🧪🧪🧪🧪

CLEAN UP 🧪

Advance Preparation

You might invite a local farmer, civil engineer, or city planner to speak to your class about food production, waste management, or planning. To help inspire students to do their best work, you might have them participate in an annual contest that awards prizes for the best design of a Mars colony. NASA, for example, has offered such a contest in the past.

Provide students with a local zoning map and several maps of Mars. The zoning map will help students see how a city is organized. The maps of Mars will help students select their colony sites. Highly detailed maps of Mars can be found on the Internet by doing a combined search of *Mars* and *map* or of *Mars* and *atlas*.

Teaching Strategies

Begin by showing the zoning map to students. Ask them why they think different parts of the city are designated for certain uses. Students should design their colony using a map scale similar to that of the zoning map. Designing a colony will be a challenge. Monitor students to be sure they understand the assignment and guide them as needed. Below are some ideas to help guide students while they develop their component.

Temperature: Just like on Earth, the coldest places on Mars are the poles. In Antarctica, scientists live in greenhouses that have many windows to trap the sun's energy. The scientists also dress warmly and use heaters. Freezing temperatures keep bacteria and fungi from breaking down organic materials. In subzero temperatures, plants lose their leaves and may die after prolonged exposure. Some animals hibernate, while others move to warmer climates. Water freezes in pipes unless the pipes are insulated or are fed by a constant supply of warm water. People trying to keep warm in freezing temperatures use a lot of electricity.

continued...

Kenneth Creese
White Mountain Junior High
Rock Springs, Wyoming

Water: On Mars, water is trapped in the northern polar icecap and possibly in the southern icecap. There may also be water in the first few centimeters of the planet's outer layer. Giant lenses could be focused on the northern polar cap to liquefy the water, which could then be transported by an insulated, heated pipeline to the colony. Ice could also be mined and transported to the colony to be melted there.

Air: Carbon dioxide, CO_2, is available in small amounts in the atmosphere and in large amounts at the South Pole (as dry ice). Colonists could use plants to photosynthesize the atmospheric CO_2 into oxygen. Plants would also have a steady supply of CO_2 from colonists' exhalation. Until sufficient vegetation was established, however, colonists would need a supply of air.

Food: Nuts, beans, and products from soybeans—such as tofu and tempeh—are high in protein and require fewer resources to grow than cattle or sheep require. Vine plants, such as grapes and peas, and most vegetables can be grown in limited space. Plants require nutrients (such as nitrogen, potassium, and phosphorus), carbon dioxide, water, and sunlight to survive. Certain soil bacteria are important for the decomposition of organic matter.

Electricity: Nuclear, wind, solar, and hydroelectric energy could be used on Mars. Nuclear generators produce a lot of energy but also a lot of toxic waste. Windmills would need to be large because of the thin atmosphere on Mars. Solar cells or panels produce a lot of energy but must be kept clean to be efficient. Water turbines require flowing water. Windmills or very large solar panels would be the most environmentally friendly generators.

A rough sketch depicting all the basic components is sufficient. After the activity, discuss what students learned by asking the following:

- What characteristics of Mars made it a challenge to develop a self-sustaining environment that supports human life?

- What opportunities for development did students find on Mars that are not available on Earth?

Evaluation Strategies

For help evaluating this lab, see the Rubric for Reports and Presentations and the Checklist for the Group Evaluation of Cooperative Group Activity in the *Assessment Checklists & Rubrics*. These resources are available in the *Classroom Management CD-ROM*.

Suggested Pacing Guide

Day 1	Days 2–3
Class is divided into teams of 4–8 students. Each team member chooses a component of the colony to design. Individually, members answer the questions for their component and sketch a simple design in their ScienceLog.	Team members combine their ideas, develop a recycling program and sketch their plan on butcher paper. Students present their drawings. Students do peer evaluations.

ECOLAB

16 **STUDENT WORKSHEET**

DESIGN YOUR OWN

There's a Space for Us

To: Dr. Ino Best, President of Arcotowns, Inc.
From: Dr. Noelle Deuitt, Director of Space Management
        International Union of Nations

Thanks to arcologically conscious companies like yours, we have made the most of the limited space on our planet. Unfortunately, the ever-increasing human population will exceed Earth's capacity in less than 15 years. We have no choice but to begin moving people to colonies beyond Earth. Mars is our first destination. Gather your best team of arcologists to design a colony. Except for the initial supplies, all materials must be from Mars. Consider the following as you design the colony: water supply, air supply, temperature control, source of energy, waste management, and food production. I trust that your arcologists can build an award-winning, life-sustaining colony.

USEFUL TERMS

arcology
a combined study of ecology and architecture

MATERIALS

- map of Mars
- city zoning map
- food group chart
- markers
- large sheet of butcher paper

Objective

Design a colony on Mars that sustains a population of humans.

Brainstorm

Each member of your team will find a way to supply one of the following to the colony: water, air, food, and electricity.

1. With your team, review the table below. Discuss how the conditions on Mars might affect each component of the colony. For example, what problems will the temperature ranges present? Record your ideas in your ScienceLog.

2. Find a suitable location on Mars for your colony. You may want to consider temperatures and potential water sources. Mark your colony's planned location on a map of Mars.

Comparing Mars and Earth

	Mars	Earth
Atmosphere	carbon dioxide: 95.3% nitrogen: 2.7% argon: 1.6% oxygen: 0.1%	nitrogen: 78% oxygen: 21%
Temperature	−133°C (winter polar regions) to 20°C (summer at the equator)	−88°C (winter in polar regions) to 58°C (summer in tropical regions)
Gravity	0.38 times that of Earth	1 G
Wind speed	0–25 km/h (average 7 km/h)	0–169 km/h
Surface	The surface contains iron, silicate minerals, radioactive potassium, uranium, and thorium.	The crust is made of mostly silicate minerals, aluminum, magnesium, and many radioactive isotopes.

Devise a Plan

Find the instructions for your component in steps 3–6, and answer the corresponding questions.

3. **Water:** Develop a plan to supply water to the colony. Write the plan in your ScienceLog. Mars will be your only source of water and materials. Assume that you will have enough electricity. As you develop your plan, consider the following questions:
   - Where are the sources of water on Mars? Identify these water sources on a map. In what physical state is the water?
   - How will you extract and store the water? What materials will you need to accomplish this task?
   - How might the temperatures on Mars affect the transportation of the water?
   - Mars has a very limited water supply. How will colonists conserve and recycle water? How will it be purified for drinking?

4. **Air:** In your ScienceLog, plan a way to produce air and supply air to the colony. With the exception of what you bring with you initially, all of your materials must come from Mars. Assume that you will have enough electricity. As you develop your plan, consider the following questions:
   - How does the atmosphere on Mars differ from the atmosphere on Earth?
   - What materials or equipment will you need to create a breathable atmosphere?
   - How could you use some of Mars's resources to make a breathable atmosphere? (Hint: Read the definitions at left.)
   - How will colonists conserve and recycle air?
   - What supplies will you bring from Earth to the colony site?

5. **Food production:** In your ScienceLog, plan a way to produce food for the colonists. The food produced on Mars must meet all of the colonists' nutritional needs. You may bring an initial supply of seeds, plants, animals, and fertilizer, but you must then rely on materials from Mars. Remember that you have a limited amount of space on the transport and in the colony. Assume that you will have enough electricity and sunlight (a day on Mars is almost as long as a day on Earth). As you develop your plan, consider the following questions:
   - What are examples of healthy foods in each of the basic food groups?
   - Will your colonists be meat-eaters or vegetarians?
   - How will you make sure plants get what they need in order to survive?
   - What supplies will you bring from Earth to the colony site?

USEFUL TERMS

photosynthesis
the process by which plants use carbon dioxide and light to make food and oxygen

electrolysis
a process that uses electricity to separate water into hydrogen and oxygen

---

EARTH SCIENCE

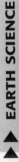

There's a Space for Us, continued

6. **Electricity:** In your ScienceLog, plan a way to supply electricity to the colony. Your team members may be relying on ample energy supplies for components of the colony. You may use only energy sources available on Mars. As you develop your plan, consider the following questions:
   - What are the potential energy sources on Mars?
   - What are the advantages and disadvantages of each source?
   - What equipment will be needed to generate electricity? How could this equipment be built from Mars's available resources?
   - Where is the best place to put the electric generator?
   - What supplies will you bring from Earth to the colony site?

Put It All Together

USEFUL TERMS

recyclable
can be processed for reuse

biodegradable
can be broken down by living organisms

nondegradable
not biodegradable and often not recyclable

7. **Develop a waste management system.** As a team, plan a way to handle the waste generated by the colony. As you develop your plan, consider the following questions:
   - What items will be recyclable? Which will be biodegradable? Which will be nondegradable?
   - What kind of facilities will colonists need for recycling?
   - Could materials decompose on Mars? Explain.
   - How will you deal with each of the following problems: packaging, toxic waste, nondegradable materials, water pollution, and air pollution.
   - How will you dispose of waste?

   Provide input to a designated recorder who will write a short report describing how waste will be managed.

8. **Draw your colony.** As a team, sketch a rough design of your colony. Keep the following things in mind:
   - How big will your colony be? How can you make the best use of the land?
   - How will you zone for domestic and industrial use?
   - What important services, such as medical, fire, and educational, will you include?
   - What kinds of recreational areas will you provide for the colonists? (Remember, gravity on Mars is one-third that of Earth!)
   - How much open space will you include in your design? Why is open space needed?
   - What type of transportation will be used in the colony?
   - How will you assure that there will be room for future growth?

   Check your sketch to be sure you've included everything. Sketch your final plan on a large piece of butcher paper.

Ozone News Zone

Cooperative Learning Activity

Group size: 3–4 students

Group goal: Inform and educate the community about the benefits and hazards of ozone.

Positive interdependence: Each group member should choose a role, such as research coordinator, recorder, discussion leader, or presentation coordinator.

Individual accountability: After the activity, students should be able to give detailed answers to questions about ozone.

Time Required

Four to six 45-minute class periods. A suggested pacing guide is provided on page 72.

Lab Ratings

EASY ————————————→ HARD

TEACHER PREP

STUDENT SET-UP

CONCEPT LEVEL

CLEAN UP

Advance Preparation

You may reduce research time and increase the time available for developing news segments by providing research materials. Obtain an audio or video recorder. Some parents may volunteer to bring and operate a video camera. You may wish to prepare a poster with the newscast title for the camera.

Safety Information

Scissors and sharp tools should be handled with care.

Teaching Strategies

On the first day, assign each group one of the following topics:
- Ozone and its chemical properties
- The importance of the ozone layer (stratospheric ozone) to Earth's ecosystems

- The causes of and remedies for our shrinking ozone layer
- Ground-level ozone—its formation and its effects
- Ozone Action Days—definition, causes, and impact on our activities

Look for the following basic information in group presentations:

General information about ozone:
While most oxygen molecules in our atmosphere consist of two oxygen atoms (O_2), ozone molecules are made of three oxygen atoms (O_3). Most atmospheric ozone is located in the stratosphere, also called "the *ozone layer*. Ozone molecules in the stratosphere absorb ultraviolet radiation from the sun, shielding Earth from approximately 90 percent of the sun's ultraviolet (UV) radiation.

The importance of the ozone layer:
Without the ozone layer, dangerous levels of UV radiation would reach Earth's lower atmosphere, causing lower crop yields and an increase in health problems such as skin cancer, eye damage, and immune suppression. Phytoplankton levels in the ocean would decrease, which would affect the food chain. Atmospheric carbon dioxide levels would rise, contributing to global warming.

continued...

Clayton Cook
Douglas Junior High
Willis, California

PHYSICAL SCIENCE

The depletion of the ozone layer: Ozone in the stratosphere is normally produced and destroyed at approximately the same rate. However, when chlorofluorocarbons (CFCs) reach the stratosphere, UV radiation breaks down the CFC molecules, releasing chlorine atoms, which destroy ozone. Chlorine destroys ozone faster than it can be generated. Since ozone depletion was first detected in the 1970s, many countries (including the United States) have taken steps to curb CFC usage on a global scale. If current regulations are followed, the ozone layer should repair itself in about 50 years.

Ground-level ozone: Ground-level ozone, the primary component of smog, is formed from chemical reactions involving sunlight, nitrogen oxides, and hydrocarbons (which are produced by motor exhaust, gasoline vapors, and industrial emissions). Ground-level ozone can be carried hundreds of miles by strong winds. It poses serious health hazards to humans, including coughing, headaches, lung damage, and irritation to the eyes, nose, and throat. In the United States, ground-level ozone causes more than $500 million worth of damage to crops each year.

Ozone Action Days: Weather conditions conducive to the formation of ground-level ozone include temperatures above

Oxygen Versus Ozone

Diatomic oxygen (O_2)	Ozone (O_3)
• colorless gas • odorless • essential to living organisms	• blue gas • sharp, pungent odor • highly toxic to both plants and animals

32°C, sunny skies, and little wind. On Ozone Action Days—days when these conditions are predicted—people are asked to limit ozone-increasing activities, such as driving, using gasoline-powered equipment, and using oil-based paints, solvents, or varnishes. People are encouraged to walk, bike, use public transportation, or carpool. In many cities, public transportation is free on Ozone Action Days.

Evaluation Strategies

For help evaluating this lab, see the Checklists for Group Evaluation of Project and Teacher Evaluation of Oral Presentation found in the *Assessment Checklists & Rubrics*. These checklists are also available in the *Classroom Management CD-ROM*.

Suggested Pacing Guide

Day 1	Days 2–3	Days 4–5	Day 6
Assign teams; members choose roles. Teams discuss research goals. Teams brainstorm for ideas and begin research.	Students share findings with teams. Students write newscasts and prepare artwork and props. Students assign speaking roles and rehearse newscasts.	Teams present newscasts. Students evaluate peers and demonstrate what they have learned. Class discusses and evaluates newscasts.	Teams share news program with other classes or with members of the community.

Name _____ Date _____ Class _____

Ozone News Zone

Thirty years into the future. . .

Agent Double Oh-Oh (O_3),

Our agents have discovered that a multinational corporation has just developed and patented two new products: an SPF 8,000 sunscreen and an air-filter mask. They plan to make a fortune once the ozone layer has become so damaged that people must wear both products to safely go outside. They have hired secret agents to sabotage international agreements protecting the ozone layer, thus making the problems concerning the ozone imminent.

Your mission is to get the word out that ozone is important. To do that, you must produce a broadcast that gets this message across accurately and convinces people to protect the international agreements.

MATERIALS

- poster board
- markers
- construction paper
- scissors
- video or audio recorder
- blank videotape or audiotape

Objective

Educate and inform your community about the hazards and benefits of ozone through a news broadcast.

Brainstorm

1. As a team, prepare a newscast on an ozone-related topic assigned by your teacher. Determine what information will be important to include in your newscast by considering the following:
   - What needs to be stated in your segment of the newscast? Be sure to include scientific facts to support all statements.
   - What background information would clarify or show the importance of what you have learned?
   - What do experts say about what you have discovered? Do all of the authorities agree?
   - What additional information will make your newscast more interesting? Think about adding props, pictures, statistics, interviews, and stories of past events.

Procedure

2. **Research your assigned ozone topic.** Use a variety of sources, such as books, magazines, the Internet, and the Environmental Protection Agency.

3. **Discuss your research as a group.** Decide which information is most important and in what order you think the information should be presented.

4. **Determine the best way to present your information.** Will your newscast be given by an anchorperson or by a reporter in the field? What will each member of your group be doing during your segment of the program?

PHYSICAL SCIENCE

5. **Write your newscast.** Write a full script for your newscast. Organize the information so that it is clear, coherent, interesting, and to the point.

6. **Prepare visual aids and props for your newscast.** Gather together any pictures or graphs you have found, or make your own. Organize your props so that they will be ready and in the correct order when you need them.

7. **Rehearse your news segment.** Practice your news segment several times so that it is smooth and well organized. Let each person in your group try all parts in the segment, then assign roles.

8. **Deliver your news segment.** Your teacher will set up a video camera or an audiotape recorder. At your teacher's signal (when the tape begins to record), present your news segment to the class.

9. **Educate your community.** Air your audiotape or videotape as a public-service announcement on a school public-address system, a local radio program, or a community-access television station.

Take Note!

10. In your ScienceLog, describe one lesson you learned from each group's presentation.

Going Further

You can help your community reduce its ozone production by promoting alternative forms of transportation, such as hike-and-bike trails. Fewer people driving fewer cars will lead to less ozone pollution.

Find out what you can do to develop a hike-and-bike trail in your area. Some organizations, such as the Rails-to-Trails Conservancy, promote turning abandoned railroad tracks into hike-and-bike trails. Some good places to start are listed below.

The Bicycle Federation of America
1506 21st Street, NW, Suite 200
Washington, DC 20036

U.S. Department of Transportation
400 Seventh Street, SW
Washington, DC 20590

Rails-to-Trails Conservancy
1100 17th Street, NW, 10th Floor
Washington, DC 20036

What's the Flap All About?

Purpose

Students observe flying birds to identify the forces involved in flight and use what they learn to construct a paper glider.

Time Required

One 45-minute class period (10 to 15 minutes for observation and discussion and 30 minutes for airplane construction)

Lab Ratings

EASY ———————————→ HARD

TEACHER PREP

STUDENT SET-UP

CONCEPT LEVEL

CLEAN UP

Advance Preparation

You may wish to do this activity during a class field trip or assign it on a Friday for students to complete over the weekend. The local Audubon Society chapter will know when and where to observe birds in flight. The best places for making observations have a diversity of plant and animal life that attracts a wide variety of birds. A nature center or an aviary at a local zoo is a good alternative. You may wish to gather field guides on birds for students to use for identification. Find out which bird types are likely to be found in your region and the preferred habitat of each species.

Teaching Strategies

Students should work individually or in pairs. Tell students that they will use their observations to help them design a paper airplane.

Before the activity, review basic concepts of forces in fluids. Students should recognize that air is a fluid. Explain to students that they will have an opportunity to see how birds move through the air by manipulating forces in fluids.

Ask students to imagine a bird flapping its wings in slow motion. Ask students what pushes against the wing (air). Point out that on a downstroke, the force that the air exerts on the wings is greater than the force of gravity on the bird.

Ask students if birds flap their wings straight up and down (no). Explain that if they did, any lift produced on a downstroke would be lost on an upstroke.

Ask students how birds orient their wings as they fly. (Birds orient their wings horizontally on the downstroke but angle or retract them on the upstroke.) Explain that the flapping of the wings produces lift. A similar use of forces can be observed in the paddling of a boat. On the forward stroke, the paddle is vertical and pushes against the water. On the return stroke, the paddle lifts from the water, minimizing any opposing force.

After students make their observations, draw a bird in flight on the chalkboard. Ask students to identify the forces that act on the bird. Have students draw arrows to indicate the direction of the forces. Label the arrows as "thrust," "drag," "gravity," or "lift." Ask students what causes each force to act on a bird.

Thrust: Most birds flap their wings or glide on wind currents to move forward through the air.

Drag: Often called air resistance, this force opposes or restricts motion in a fluid. A bird's body is streamlined to reduce drag.

Gravity: Gravity pulls a bird's mass downward. The greater a bird's mass is, the greater its weight. A bird's bones contain hollow spaces that minimize weight. Birds also reduce their weight by releasing waste during takeoff.

continued...

Paul Boyle
Perry Heights Middle School
Evansville, Indiana

PHYSICAL SCIENCE

Lift: Lift is created as birds flap their wings or glide. Lift allows birds to overcome the force of their own weight.

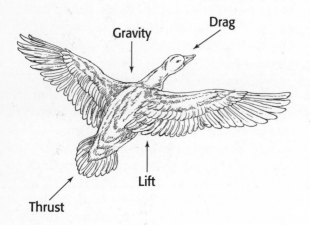

Gravity

Drag

Lift

Thrust

Lift is affected by the angle of the bird's wings and the surface of the wings. The upper wing surface, like the wing of an airplane, is curved. Air moves faster over the wing than under the wing, causing the air pressure above the wing to drop and resulting in a net force upward (Bernoulli's Principle). Students may have noticed the effect of angle on lift while holding their hand out the window of a moving car. When their hand is horizontal, the air flowing over and under the hand exerts equal and opposite forces. When the hand is angled, the air pushes the hand up or down, depending on how the air is deflected.

Although hummingbirds flap their wings continually, many birds flap only during takeoff and then glide on air currents to remain aloft. Some birds, such as condors, rely on air currents to lift them without much flapping. Ask students why all birds aren't efficient gliders. You might want to hint that bird owners clip some of their birds' feathers to prevent them from flying. *(Gliding depends mostly on the size and shape of the wing.)*

HELPFUL HINT

Show students a videotape of flying birds in slow motion. Help them identify how the flapping motion and the angle of the wings generates lift. You might also show students a humorous videotape of early human attempts at flight and have students identify the problems with each design.

Evaluation Strategies

For help evaluating this lab, see the Checklist for Self-Evaluation of Learning Skills and the Activity Observation Checklist in the *Assessment Checklists & Rubrics*. These checklist are also available in the *Classroom Management CD-ROM*.

Name _____ Date _____ Class _____

What's the Flap All About?

It's not easy working for a genius . . .

Your tutor, Leonardo DaVinci, is hatching another scheme. He has this wild idea that a human can fly like a bird. Imagine that! Unfortunately, this preoccupation with flight has stopped all of his other work. He cannot even pick up a piece of paper without folding it into a birdlike shape and sailing it through the air. How can humans fly without feathers? Has DaVinci lost his mind?

Now DaVinci is designing a flying machine, and he has asked you for help. You must go out into the field and observe birds as they take flight, soar, rise, dive, and land. Is it possible that studying these amazing creatures could unlock the secrets of flight? Master DaVinci seems to think so.

MATERIALS

- binoculars (optional)
- field guide to birds
- paper
- scissors
- tape
- glue

SAFETY ALERT!

Go with an adult to observe bird flight. Do not go alone.

USEFUL TERMS

gravity
downward force

lift
upward force

thrust
forward force

drag
backward force

Objective

Observe birds as they fly, paying careful attention to the size, shape, angle, and movement of the wings and tail; and use your observations to design a paper airplane that will glide farther than your classmates' planes.

Look Up in the Sky!

1. Your teacher will tell you where and when you can watch birds fly. A pair of binoculars and a field guide will help you with your observations.

2. At the designated place and time, watch a bird fly for 10–15 minutes. In your ScienceLog, describe the size, shape, angle, and movement of a bird's wings and tail. If you have a field guide, use it to identify the bird. Sketch the bird's body as it flies.

3. In your ScienceLog, use your sketch of the bird to draw a paper-airplane design.

4. In your ScienceLog, illustrate the forces that act on the bird. Draw arrows indicating the direction of each force. Using the terms at left, explain how these forces affect the bird as it flies. Remember, air is a fluid!

5. Use your ScienceLog drawing to build a paper airplane that will fly farther that your classmates' planes. Pay careful attention to the shape and size of the wing and tail. You may cut and paste the paper—you do not have to rely on folding.

6. When your teacher gives you the signal, line up and fly your planes. Whose plane flew the farthest? In your ScienceLog, describe how their design was different from yours.

PHYSICAL SCIENCE

Putting It All Together

7. How do birds produce thrust?

_____

8. How did your airplane produce thrust?

_____

9. How does the shape of the wings help a bird fly?

_____

_____

_____

_____

10. How do birds overcome their weight to produce lift?

_____

_____

_____

_____

_____

_____

11. After observing birds in flight and constructing a simple flying machine, what can you report back to DaVinci about the possibilities of human flight?

_____

_____

_____

Going Further

Find out why traveling in a V formation enables a flock of birds to use less energy in flight. In fact, birds flying in this formation use half the energy they would use if they were each flying solo!

Energy-Efficient Home

Purpose

Students test the insulating properties of various materials, then design a model of an energy-efficient home.

Time Required

Four 45-minute class periods

Lab Ratings

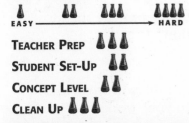

EASY ———————→ HARD

TEACHER PREP
STUDENT SET-UP
CONCEPT LEVEL
CLEAN UP

ADDITIONAL MATERIALS (PER CLASS)

Selection of the following insulating materials: sand, pebbles, clay, shredded paper, cardboard, sawdust, thick cloth, cotton batting, shredded plastic foam, feathers, wool, cellulose insulation, rock wool insulation, vermiculite, rigid foam insulation

Advance Preparation

One week before the activity, ask students to bring in empty soup cans and coffee cans with lids. Make sure that all the edges are smooth. Obtain various insulating materials at a building supply center, craft store, or garden supply store. Use a large coffee can for the large outer container and a soup can for the inner container. The nail should be slightly wider than the thermometer. Cover all workspaces with tarps. The cardboard boxes should be of various sizes so that students can incorporate the box size as a design feature.

Safety Information

Students should wear heat-resistant gloves during the first part of this activity. Heat-resistant gloves are not waterproof—caution students to be very careful when handling the hot water, or pour the hot

water for each group. Be sure hot plates have an "On-Off" switch and indicator light. Instruct students never to leave a heated hot plate unattended and never to heat water above 60°C. Do not use mercury thermometers because boiling water will break them. Use ethanol thermometers instead. Students should use caution when handling scissors.

Teaching Strategies

This activity works best with groups of 3–4 students. Have each group test a different material. At least one group should conduct a control test with no insulation. Home designs should be based on the climate in your region. For example, houses in the desert might have smaller, east- or west-facing windows with an extended roof. Houses in northern latitudes might have large, south-facing windows with no overhang. Although designs will vary, some things to look for include the following recommendations: insulate ceilings and walls; paint the house with a light color to reflect sunlight; shade the windows with thick curtains or a roof overhang; ventilate the house to allow cool outside air into the house; use lightweight materials, such as wood, paper, sawdust, and cardboard, to internally allow rooms to heat and cool quickly; caulk around windows, doors, and ceilings to control air leakage.

Evaluation Strategies

For help evaluating this lab, see the Rubric for Experiments and the Checklist for Self-Evaluation of Lesson in the *Assessment Checklists & Rubrics.* These resources are also available in the *Classroom Management CD-ROM.*

Laura Fleet
Landrum Middle School
Ponte Vedra Beach, Florida

PHYSICAL SCIENCE

EcoLab
19 **STUDENT WORKSHEET**

DESIGN YOUR OWN

Energy-Efficient Home

You are applying for a position with Sun Homes, a firm that builds attractive and energy-efficient houses in your area. To get the job, you must show Sun Homes that you know about insulators and their efficiency. As part of the interview process, you must build a model of an energy-efficient home with your insulator of choice. Sun Homes will choose the applicant with the most efficient model. Good luck!

MATERIALS

- large coffee can with plastic lid
- smaller can with a volume of at least 200 mL
- insulating material
- nail
- heat-resistant gloves
- 250 mL beaker
- water
- hot plate
- outdoor thermometer

SAFETY ALERT!

Always wear heat-resistant gloves while working with the hot plate or hot water or while disassembling the insulation tester. Do not heat the water above 60°C. Be careful not to spill hot water on yourself or others. If a thermometer breaks, notify your teacher immediately.

SCIENTIFIC METHOD

Ask a Question

Which insulating materials provide the most efficient home insulation?

Make a Prediction

1. Which insulating material do you think will work best? Select this material, and bring it to your workspace to test.

Conduct an Experiment–Part 1: Testing Insulation

2. Assemble an insulation tester as shown. Use a nail to punch a hole through the center of the plastic lid.

3. Completely fill the space between the two cans with your chosen insulation.

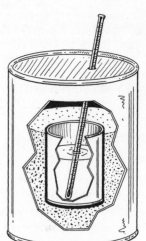

4. Put on heatproof mitts. Pour 200 mL of water into a beaker. Put the beaker on a hot plate, and heat the water to 60°C. Do not overheat the water. Water hotter than 60°C can scald.

5. Wearing heat-resistant gloves, pour the hot water into the inner can of the tester. Be very careful not to get the insulation wet.

6. Quickly seal the lid, and insert the thermometer. Immerse the bulb, but don't let it touch the bottom of the can.

7. Immediately read the water temperature, and record the results in your ScienceLog. Repeat every 5 minutes for 30 minutes.

8. If time allows, repeat steps 1–7 with another insulating material or without any insulation.

---

9. Which is a more effective insulator, tightly packed material or loosely packed material? Explain your answer.

_____

_____

_____

_____

Draw Conclusions

10. Which material would you choose to insulate a house?

_____

_____

_____

_____

MATERIALS
• scissors
• cardboard box with lid
• metric ruler
• clear plastic wrap
• transparent tape
• thermometer
• one or more of the following: caulk, paint, colored construction paper

Part 2: Model an Energy-Efficient Home

Now that you have a good idea of what materials make good insulators, build a model of an energy-efficient home. Then make a second model home, adding features to improve its insulating efficiency.

11. Cut a 5 × 5 cm window in a cardboard box. Cover the window with plastic wrap, and tape it in place. Place a thermometer in the model so that it can be seen through the window. Tape the thermometer in place.

12. Position your control model so that it faces the sun to allow the most sunlight to enter the window.

13. Record the temperature in the model at the start of this experiment and every 5 minutes for 30 minutes.

Model Home Temperatures

	Start	5 min	10 min	15 min	20 min	25 min	30 min
Control temperature (°C)							
Experimental temperature (°C)							

PHYSICAL SCIENCE

Ask a Question

14. How can you improve your home's performance?

_____

_____

_____

_____

Form a Hypothesis

15. With your group, design an energy-efficient home design that best improves your model's insulating ability. Consider the following design features:
  • location and surface area of windows
  • roof overhang
  • type of insulation
  • interior and exterior surface colors and finishes
  • air leakage around windows, doors, etc.

16. Based on your discussion, record a hypothesis in your ScienceLog about what kind of energy-efficient home will best save energy resources. Sketch your experimental model design in your ScienceLog.

Test the Hypothesis

17. After your teacher has approved your design, modify the box to build your new, improved model.

18. Repeat steps 12–13 to test your design, and record your results in the table on page 81.

Analyze the Results

In your ScienceLog, answer the following questions:

19. How do you account for any difference in the effectiveness of your two models?

20. Compare your results with the results of other groups. Were their designs more efficient? If so, what did they do differently? If you could redesign your model, what changes would you make?

Greener Cleaners

Purpose

Students test and compare eco-friendly products and commercial cleaners.

Time Required

Two 45-minute class periods

Lab Ratings

EASY ——————————→ HARD

TEACHER PREP 🧪🧪🧪

STUDENT SET-UP 🧪🧪

CONCEPT LEVEL 🧪🧪

CLEAN UP 🧪🧪🧪🧪

ADDITIONAL MATERIALS (PER CLASS)

- small tomato
- 3 tarps
- masking tape
- soiled oily white rags
- small bowl of water
- 3 large bowls
- mixing spoon
- wooden blocks (optional)

Advance Preparation

The materials listed on page 84 are enough for an entire class. Set up four stations as indicated below.

Station Setup

Cleaner	Station
General cleaner	Smash a tomato on a tabletop or counter top. Let it dry.
Fabric stain remover	Place rags beside a sink. Cover the floor nearby.
Window cleaner	Cover the floor under a classroom window or mirror.
Furniture polish	Cover the floor under a piece of wooden furniture, or some wooden blocks.

Safety Information

Students should wear an apron, goggles, and protective gloves at all times. Conduct this activity in a well-ventilated area. Students with respiratory problems should not do this lab. Students should read and follow the warning labels on all cleaning products. Students should not touch their face or mucous membranes. Keep all chemicals away from heat. Spilled liquid on floors is hazardous.

Teaching Strategies

This activity works best when groups of 4–5 students rotate through the stations. Before the activity, discuss why some cleaning products are hazardous. Explain that most commercial cleaners contain strong acids or bases. Tell students to look on labels for prefixes such as *naphtha, benz-, chloro-,* and *oxal-* to help them identify harmful products. Point out that both commercial and "green" cleaners can be hazardous. Students should not get lemon juice, vinegar, or baking soda in their eyes.

Evaluation Strategies

For help evaluating this lab, see the Checklist for Teacher Evaluation of Lesson and the Activity Observation Checklist in the *Assessment Checklists & Rubrics*. These checklists are also available in the *Classroom Management CD-ROM*.

Laura Fleet
Landrum Middle School
Ponte Vedra Beach, Florida

PHYSICAL SCIENCE

EcoLab

20   **STUDENT WORKSHEET**

DISCOVERY LAB

Greener Cleaners

Announcer: Welcome to the *Greenest House on the Block Contest!* We are all excited to see how many contestants have stepped up to the challenge of not only conserving water, energy, and resources by recycling but also switching to Earth-friendly cleaners. Let's talk to some contestants. Mr. Vinny Garr, from Plum Street, how will you clean your home without using commercial cleaners?

Mr. Garr: Well, I figure I'll use a little baking soda, lemon juice, vinegar and, oh, a lot of elbow grease. Heh, heh!

Announcer: Amazing conviction, sir. Good luck to you. Here's Ms. Emma Scour. Ms. Scour, won't the convenience of commercial cleaners be a big temptation?

Ms. Scour: Not really. Just look at the money I'll save while protecting my health and the health of our planet. If it's important to keep our houses clean, it should be just as important to keep our Earth clean. After all, it's our home too!

Announcer: Attitudes like these make me proud to be green! Let's wish these families luck as they "go for the green" in our *Greenest House on the Block Contest!*

MATERIALS

- protective gloves
- 4 L of white vinegar
- 1 L of lemon juice
- box of baking soda
- water
- scouring pads, steel wool, toothbrushes
- general cleaner
- fabric stain remover
- chalk
- spray bottle
- newspaper
- window cleaner
- 1 L of vegetable oil
- cleaning rags
- furniture polish
- buckets
- pH test paper
- measuring cups and spoons

Objective

Investigate alternatives to hazardous household cleansers.

Try an Alternative

1. Go to a station, and prepare the eco-friendly cleanser according to the instructions in the table below.

How to Prepare Greener Cleaners

General cleaner	• Treat stains with undiluted white vinegar or lemon juice. • Make a paste of baking soda and water for scouring.
Fabric stain remover	• To remove grease: rub on chalk, let set, then wash. • To clean whites: soak in baking soda solution, and wash.
Window cleaner	• Mix 60 mL of white vinegar in 1 L of water. Spray on the windows, and then wipe dry with newspaper.
Furniture polish	• Mix 30 mL vegetable oil and 15 mL of white vinegar, and slowly stir into 1 L of water.

Greener Cleaners, continued

2. Use the eco-friendly product on a portion of the test area until the product has done its job as well as possible.

3. Use the commercial product on another portion of the test area until the product has done its job as well as possible.

4. Repeat steps 1–3 until you have been to all four stations. In your ScienceLog, note the effectiveness of the product at each station.

You Be the Judge

5. Which of the eco-friendly ingredients have acidic properties? (Hint: You can find out by touching pH paper to the cleaner.)

_____

6. Which of the eco-friendly ingredients have properties of bases? (Hint: You can find out by touching pH paper to the cleaner.)

_____

7. Which of the eco-friendly ingredients have absorbent properties?

_____

8. Which of the eco-friendly ingredients have abrasive properties?

_____

9. How do you think these cleaners work?

_____

_____

_____

_____

_____

_____

_____

_____

_____

PHYSICAL SCIENCE

_____

Greener Cleaners, continued
_____

10. How did the acids, bases, or abrasives in eco-friendly cleaners compare in strength with the ingredients often contained in commercial products? Explain.

_____

_____

_____

_____

11. Would you use eco-friendly cleaners instead of commercial cleaners? Explain your answer.

_____

_____

_____

_____

_____

12. Are eco-friendly cleaners always safe?

_____

_____

_____

Critical Thinking

13. Many household cleaners are sold in unnecessary or nonrecyclable packaging. How could you cut down on excess packaging?

_____

_____

_____

_____

_____

_____

DISCOVERY LAB

A Light Current of Air

Purpose

Students build a device that uses wind energy to produce enough electricity to light an LED (light emitting diode).

Time Required

Three 45-minute class periods

Lab Ratings

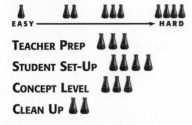

EASY ——————→ HARD

TEACHER PREP

STUDENT SET-UP

CONCEPT LEVEL

CLEAN UP

Advance Preparation

Enameled wire is also known as AWG 36 magnet wire. Any cardboard box with a width of 8.5 cm can substitute for the shoe box. Try to use a blow dryer with a fan (cold air) setting. Pencils should be smooth and round and have the same diameter as the hole. Use new pencils to provide a flat surface to affix the magnet onto. Cut a 10 × 10 cm posterboard square for each group. On each square, draw the turbine pattern shown. Make sure the hole is in the center of each square or the windmill may not work properly. The cuts should be no closer to the center hole than 0.5 cm. The success of this lab depends heavily on the speed of rotation, the strength of the magnet, and the geometry of the magnetic field lines and wire coils. Therefore, do not substitute materials unless you test the lab first and are certain that it will work. Because the wire is thin, do not use wire strippers; burn the enamel from the ends of the wire.

Safety Information

Do not allow students to use electrical equipment near water or wet surfaces or with wet hands. A dryer without a fan-only setting may be used, but the blow dryer will heat the tack. Caution students not to touch the hot tack.

Teaching Strategies

This activity works best with groups of 3–6 students. Begin by showing pictures of windmills. Remind students that a windmill requires a large surface area to catch the wind but that it should weigh as little as possible to be efficient. Show students how to use a voltmeter or a multimeter.

After the activity, explain that we usually get electricity from electric generating plants that use steam, wind, or falling water from a dam to rotate the fan blades of a turbine. The rotating turbine shaft turns a magnet and coil, called the generator. The steam may be produced by using the heat from burning fossil fuels, burning biomass, or nuclear reactions.

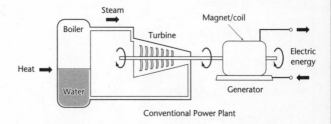

Conventional Power Plant

Evaluation Strategies

For help evaluating this lab, see the Checklist for Self-Evaluation of Lesson and the Activity Observation Checklist in the *Assessment Checklists & Rubrics*. These checklists are also available in the *Classroom Management CD-ROM*.

CLASSROOM TESTED & APPROVED

Paul Boyle
Perry Heights Middle School
Evansville, Indiana

PHYSICAL SCIENCE

EcoLab

21 **STUDENT WORKSHEET**

A Light Current of Air

The bayside community of Pier's End is losing tourism due to the recent energy conservation ordinance decreed by the town council. This town is famous for its kilometer-long boardwalk with many colored lights; it is a perfect place for midnight strolls. Since the ordinance went into effect, the lights have to be off by 8 P.M. each evening, leaving many strolling couples in the dark.

So far, the best option is to close the pier after 8 P.M., when the lights are out. But, this would turn away many tourists who come to shop near the boardwalk area in the evening. As the newly appointed Parks and Recreation Director, you have an idea that will brighten up things around the boardwalk and still conserve energy. Around the bay there is plenty of wind all the time. If you could harness all of that tremendous wind power with a series of windmills, you might be able to conserve energy and bring back the tourists at the same time!

MATERIALS

- 10 × 10 cm poster-board square with turbine pattern
- scissors
- hole punch
- round pencil
- thumbtack
- transparent tape
- shoe box
- metric ruler
- 2 pipe cleaners
- ALNICO cow magnet
- 229 m of enameled wire
- 500 g of modeling clay
- 2 alligator clips and wire
- voltmeter or multimeter
- 1500 W, 60 Hz blow dryer
- 2.0 V LED

Objective

Build a device that uses wind energy to produce enough electricity to light a light emitting diode (LED).

Catch the Wind

1. Cut out the turbine. Punch a hole in the center only and cut along the lines almost to the center.

2. Slide the turbine onto the eraser end of the pencil; bend the flaps of the turbine toward the eraser, and attach them with a thumbtack. The turbine should rotate freely when blown on.

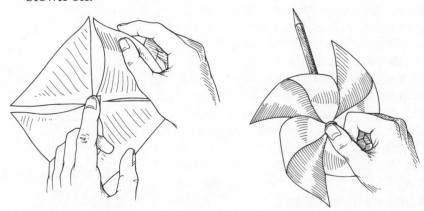

3. Tape the back end of the turbine to the pencil so that the turbine can no longer rotate unless the pencil rotates with it. Allow lots of space between the front and back ends to catch wind.

4. Place the box on the table so that the opening faces up. Measure 7 cm above the table on a long side of the box, and mark that point. Punch a hole through the point.

A Light Current of Air, continued

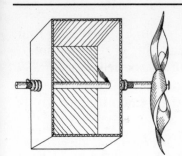

5. Repeat step 4 on the opposite side of the box so the holes are aligned.

6. Attach the box to the table, or place a weight inside the box. Slide the pencil through the two holes so the pencil points horizontally and the turbine hangs over the table's edge. Allow 4 cm of pencil to hang out on the turbine side of the box.

7. Wrap pipe cleaners around the pencil where it exits the box on both sides. Tape the pipe cleaners to the pencil.

8. Tape the magnet to the eraser end of the pencil so that the pencil and magnet form a T, as shown. The two poles of the magnet should stick out to the left and right.

9. Place the coiled wire beside the magnet. Point the magnet's pole to the center of the coil. Use the modeling clay to adjust the height of the coil so that the center of the coil is the same height as the magnet when it points to the coil.

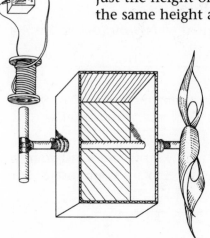

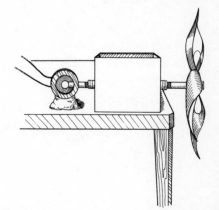

HELPFUL HINT

A good connection between the wires, the stable rotation of the turbine, and the wire coil being very close to the magnet will ensure that the windmill works.

10. Find the two loose ends of the wire—one wire is inside the coil and the other wire is outside the coil. Tape the outside of the coil so that it doesn't unravel. Connect each loose wire end to a separate alligator clip and wire assembly. Clip the loose end of each alligator clip and wire assembly to a different voltmeter terminal.

11. Direct the blow dryer on the turbine. For best results, hold the blow dryer at an angle, as shown on the next page. Do not point directly at the center of the turbine but at one of the blades from the side. As the turbine spins, read the voltage on the voltmeter.

12. Adjust the wire spool and the spinning magnet so that they are as close together as possible.

PHYSICAL SCIENCE

A Light Current of Air, continued

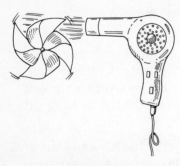

Correct

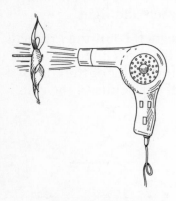

Incorrect

13. If the magnet or pencil wobbles as it spins, adjust it so that one end of the pencil points to the center of the magnet. Also adjust the pipe cleaners around the pencil; just a slight movement can change how much the magnet wobbles. Be patient; the alignment must be exact for the windmill to produce electricity.

14. Once the voltmeter consistently shows over 1 V, disconnect the voltmeter, and clip the alligator clips and wire assembly to each wire of an LED.

15. Repeat steps 11–13 so that the LED glows. Wow! You've just run a small light using a wind-powered generator.

16. Repeat steps 11–13 so that the LED glows again. Now, rotate the coil so that the rotating magnet points in the same direction as the coil.

Analyze the Results

17. What happened when you rotated the coil? Why?

_____

_____

_____

18. Why would you want to use wind energy instead of other forms of energy? Explain your answer.

_____

_____

_____

_____

19. What are some of the disadvantages of using wind energy?

_____

_____

_____

20. How might you solve these problems?

_____

_____

_____

A Light Current of Air, continued

21. In this activity, the wind that drives the windmills is probably not a renewable source of energy. Why is this true?

_____

_____

_____

_____

22. For what other purposes could you use the rotation of a turbine?

_____

_____

_____

_____

23. List other ways to move the turbine.

_____

_____

_____

_____

24. If the wind isn't blowing, and you have a choice of burning coal or biomass to generate electricity, which would you choose? Explain.

_____

_____

_____

Going Further

Have you ever seen someone push-start a car after the battery has been discharged? Explain in your ScienceLog how pushing the car helps start it.

PHYSICAL SCIENCE

▲
▲
▲

An Earful of Sounds

Purpose

Students record and study different sounds to define noise pollution.

Time Required

Two 45-minute class periods

Lab Ratings

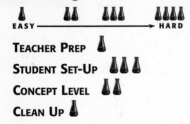

EASY ——————————→ HARD

TEACHER PREP

STUDENT SET-UP

CONCEPT LEVEL

CLEAN UP

Advance Preparation

Obtain five or six tape recorders for the in-class portion of the activity. You may wish to have students bring in tape recorders. Earplugs can be obtained at a drugstore and should be provided for the students' protection while they are recording sounds. Have extra batteries on hand.

Safety Information

Students should not use electrical equipment with wet hands or near water.

Teaching Strategies

This activity works best with groups of 2–4 students. Ask students to define noise pollution. Have they been to a concert at which they needed earplugs? How loud do they normally listen to stereos? Discuss how some sounds can damage hearing. The intensity level of a sound is measured in decibels (dB). People risk hearing loss at noise levels above 85 dB, yet many rock concerts register levels over 110 dB.

Before forming groups, ask which students have portable tape recorders (not tape players) at home. Group students who don't have tape recorders with students who do. Be sure students understand the difference between loudness and pitch. *(Loudness is how loud or soft a sound is. Pitch is the highness or lowness of a sound.)* Too many different sounds can be just as irritating as one loud sound. You might need to show students how to write a mirror image of their name.

Evaluation Strategies

For help evaluating this lab, see the Checklist for Self-Evaluation of Cooperative Group Activity in the *Assessment Checklists & Rubrics*. This checklist is also available in the *Classroom Management CD-ROM*. You may also find the following grading scale helpful:

Grading Scale

Possible points	Originality (50 points possible)
50–25	Sounds selected reflect creative thought and imagination and are appropriate for the objective and theme of this lab.
25–0	Sounds selected reflect creative thought and imagination but are inappropriate for the objective and theme of this lab.
Possible points	Quantity (50 points possible)
50–0	Award 2 points for each sound recorded.

Paul Boyle
Perry Heights Middle School
Evansville, Indiana

FIELD ACTIVITY

22 **STUDENT WORKSHEET**

DESIGN
YOUR OWN

An Earful of Sounds

You are a composer and a master of 15 different instruments, including your own voice. Usually, you are the toast of the town, but lately you have been accused of noise pollution!

Perhaps the accusations have something to do with your new "musical" pieces, which use recordings of everyday sounds against a musical background. What's *wrong* with your Car Horn Sonata and your Cuckoo Clock Concerto? They're not loud; they're just different!

Well, maybe your music *does* pollute a little. But if you could figure out what noise pollution is, you could make your music more soothing to the untrained ear.

After writing down all the sounds from your musical pieces, you try to think of sounds that others might find pleasing. Then you decide to compile a collection of sounds by doing a sound scavenger hunt!

You had better hurry! You play in Carnegie Hall in 2 weeks!

MATERIALS

- tape recorder
- blank cassette tape
- 2–4 pairs of earplugs
- various objects that make sound
- 2 batteries

SAFETY ALERT!

Protect your hearing! Wear earplugs while recording loud noises.

USEFUL TERMS

loudness
how loud or soft a sound is

pitch
the highness or lowness of a sound

Objective

Observe and record sounds in different environments to formulate a personal definition of noise pollution.

A Scavenger Hunt of Sounds

1. Review the Sounds Checklist on page 94. As a group, add five more sounds that you think others would find pleasing (e.g., the purring of a cat).

2. Decide where to find these sounds. Divide the list, and assign part of the list to each group member.

3. **At home:** Record at least 10–30 seconds of each sound. Place a check in the box beside each item recorded. Pack your cassette tape in your bag to bring to class.

4. In the table on page 94, indicate the loudness and pitch of each sound.

5. **In class:** On a separate sheet of paper, sign your full name.

6. Play the taped recordings. As you listen, write a mirror image of your signature. Do any sounds make it difficult to concentrate on this task? Do any sounds help you concentrate?

7. Fill out the last column on page 94 for every sound.

8. In your ScienceLog, list the sounds that you would like included in your symphony.

9. What sounds cannot be included in your symphony? Describe those sounds in your ScienceLog.

PHYSICAL SCIENCE

Sounds Checklist

✔	Source	Loudness (loud, medium, soft)	Pitch (high, medium, low)	Feeling (irritating, neutral, calming)
	honking horn			
	large motor vehicle (bus, boat, truck)			
	flying insect (fly, bee, mosquito)			
	fast-moving stream or river			
	wind			
	rain			
	thunder			
	chirping birds			
	barking dog			
	crickets			
	construction (hammering, sawing, drilling)			
	clock			
	musical instrument (not a band)			
	electronic device (printer, computer, copier)			
	whistle			
	bell(s)			
	a ringing telephone			
	smoke alarm (let your parents help you with this)			
	airplane			
	appliance (vacuum cleaner, dishwasher, etc.)			

An Earful of Sounds, continued

Sound Off!

10. Look over your list of responses on page 94 and think about what certain sounds might have in common. Is there a pattern to the types of sounds you found irritating or calming? Explain your answer.

_____

_____

_____

_____

11. What is your definition of noise pollution?

_____

_____

_____

_____

12. Based on your observations, what types of sounds do you feel contribute most to noise pollution?

_____

_____

_____

_____

Critical Thinking

13. What could be done in your community to reduce noise pollution?

_____

_____

_____

_____

_____

PHYSICAL SCIENCE

Photon Drive

Purpose

Students construct a solar car to learn about alternative fuel sources.

Time Required

One 45-minute class period

Lab Ratings

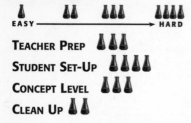

EASY ————————→ HARD

TEACHER PREP

STUDENT SET-UP

CONCEPT LEVEL

CLEAN UP

Advance Preparation

Obtain the materials from an electronic store, discount store, craft store, or scientific supply house. This lab was tested using the 3 V Mabuchi "Cer-Mag" model RE 280 motor, which is widely available in electronic stores. Although hot glue facilitates the assembly, wood glue is stronger, lighter, and safer. On a cloudy day, you may wish to have a flashlight or a portable lamp on hand so that students can test their cars indoors. Make a "start" and a "finish" line in a large, flat clear area, such as a gymnasium floor. You may choose to make a sample car in advance to use as a model.

Safety Information

Students should use extreme caution while using sharp objects. They should wear eye protection. Do not allow students to use a hot glue gun.

Teaching Strategies

This lab works best with groups of 2–4 students. Before the activity, explain how a solar car works. The solar panel is the power source for the car. The solar cells convert light into electricity. The solar panel is made of two special materials called *semiconductors*. When these two unique materials are put together in a sandwich form, electrons are attracted to the top half of the sandwich but not enough to move. The sunlight shining on the semiconductors delivers enough energy to free the electrons, allowing them to move to the top of the sandwich. When wires connect the panel to a motor, electrons move through the wire into the motor, making it spin, and back through another wire to the solar panel to fill the empty spaces. The more light the panel collects, the more electricity that is produced.

The key to having the car move in a straight path is to add enough modeling clay to balance the weight of the motor. The mass of the modeling clay should be almost the same as the mass of the motor. To make the solar panel more efficient, keep the panel clean. Dirt and dust block sunlight. Solar cells work better when kept cool. Reflectors can be added on each side of the solar cells to direct more light to the cell, as shown.

Evaluation Strategies

For help evaluating this lab, see the Checklists for the Observation of Cooperative Group and Self-Evaluation of Cooperative Group Activity in the *Assessment Checklists & Rubrics*. These checklists are also available in the *Classroom Management CD-ROM*.

Laura Fleet
Landrum Middle School
Ponte Vedra Beach, Florida

ECOLAB

23 **STUDENT WORKSHEET**

Photon Drive

The people have spoken! They are tired of parking meters, ridiculous parking fees, and awful lunch-time traffic! Buses solve half the problem, but what if you need to get from one side of downtown to the other in a hurry? Buses still get stuck in the noon-time traffic and they still pollute.

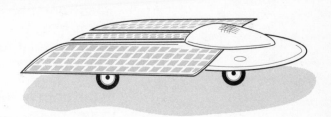

What a great opportunity for your mass transit company! You have recently decided to merge with a small solar energy company to develop a solar-powered tram. This car, called the *Arrow Transport,* would travel separate routes from one side of town to the other with stops in between. The system would reduce downtown traffic, pollution, and parking hassles.

Your company has put in a bid, but you must still compete with several other providers to get the contract. The city council will choose only the fastest and straightest-traveling vehicle for this project! You have until their meeting tomorrow to create your prototype. Good luck!

MATERIALS

- tongue depressor
- scissors
- plastic drinking straw
- bamboo skewer
- metric ruler
- 3 film canister lids
- 2 pencil erasers
- wood glue
- 1.5 V–3.0 V motor
- rubber bands
- hook-and-loop adhesive tape
- sheet of corrugated cardboard
- solar cells
- modeling clay
- 5 insulated wires with alligator clips
- aluminum foil

Objective

Construct a solar car to explore the use of an alternative fuel.

Procedure

1. Cut the tongue depressor to three-fourths its original length. This will serve as the body of the car.

2. Cut the straw in half. Pull the loose fibers from the bamboo skewer to reduce friction, and place it inside the straw. Cut the bamboo skewer so that it is 2.5 cm longer than the straw piece. This will serve as the axle of the car.

3. Make tiny holes in the center of two of the film canister lids for the rear wheels. Pull the erasers off two new pencils. Connect a lid to each end of the bamboo skewer, and secure the lids in place with the erasers.

4. Glue the axle to one end of the tongue depressor so that it forms a T, as shown at left.

5. Mount the motor sideways on the other end of the tongue depressor, as shown. The motor shaft should be mounted so that it is parallel to the bamboo skewer at the opposite end.

PHYSICAL SCIENCE

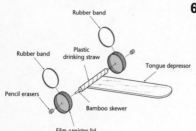

6. Cut a tiny hole in the middle of the third lid. Push the lid snugly onto the motor shaft so that it spins evenly. Glue the lid to the shaft to serve as the front drive wheel of the car. Center the front drive wheel in the front of the car. Tightly mount rubber bands on the wheels' edges to provide added traction.

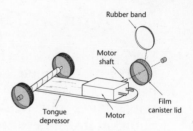

7. Congratulations! The car should now be able to roll along the floor supported by three wheels. No parts should drag.

8. Use hook-and-loop adhesive tape to mount the four solar cells side-by-side on the cardboard square, as shown. Then connect the solar cells with wires, as shown.

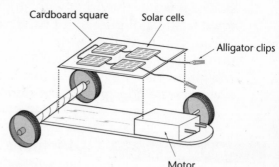

9. Use rubber bands to mount the solar cell unit on top of the tongue depressor. Use alligator clips to connect the free ends of the wires to the posts of the motor, as shown below.

10. Add enough modeling clay to the cardboard on the side opposite the motor to ensure that the car runs in a straight line.

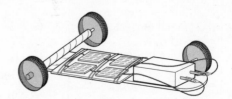

Analysis

11. How could you modify your solar car to make it faster?

_____

_____

_____

12. Modify your car so that it goes faster. Place your car on the starting line. At your teacher's mark, start your car and let it travel to the finish line.

Photon Drive, continued

13. Compare the performance of your car with that of the other cars in the class. Whose car went the fastest and the straightest? How did the designs of your classmates differ from yours?

_____

_____

_____

Critical Thinking

14. When automobiles burn gasoline, the combustion process leads to the creation of small amounts of ozone, a highly reactive form of oxygen, which is a main component of smog. What advantages does a solar car have over a gasoline-powered automobile?

_____

_____

_____

_____

15. What problems prevent us from making all cars solar?

_____

_____

_____

_____

_____

16. How could these problems be solved?

_____

_____

_____

PHYSICAL SCIENCE

Name _____ Date _____ Class _____

Water Wigglers, continued

20. What features were most helpful in grouping the organisms?

Sample answer: Features such as shape, size, means of mobility, and color were most helpful in grouping the organisms.

_____

_____

_____

Critical Thinking

21. How would you change your classification system to be able to identify other kinds of organisms?

Sample answer: I would add new categories or modify the

existing ones.

_____

_____

22. Study the picture below. Did you see any of these organisms? Circle the organisms you saw under the microscope.

Art Credits

All art, unless otherwise noted, by Holt, Rinehart and Winston.

5 (bc), Carlyn Iverson; 12 (bl), Layne Lundstrom; 15 (cr), David Chapman; 23 (bc), Carlyn Iverson; 44 (tr), Layne Lundstrom; 49 (tr), Accurate Art, Inc.; 57 (tr), David Chapman; 57 (br), David Chapman; 60 (br), Accurate Art, Inc.; 76 (tl), Laurie O'Keefe; 77 (tr), Laurie O'Keefe; 80 (cr), Carlyn Iverson; 81 (cr), Accurate Art, Inc; 87 (bl), Carlyn Iverson; 87 (cr), Accurate Art, Inc; 88 (br), Carlyn Iverson; 88 (bl), Carlyn Iverson; 89 (tl), Carlyn Iverson; 89 (c), Carlyn Iverson; 89 (cr), Carlyn Iverson; 90 (tl), Carlyn Iverson; 96 (tl), Accurate Art, Inc.

Answer Key

EcoLabs & Field Activities

· CONTENTS ·

Water Wigglers, continued

23. In a dictionary, look up the names of the organisms listed in the table below. What is the connection between an organism's name and its characteristics? For each organism in the table fill in the word root(s), meaning(s), and the connection between the name and the organism's characteristics.

Organism Names and Meanings

Name	Root(s)	Meaning	Connection
Actinophrys	aktinos	rays	it seems to have rays coming out of its body
Amoeba	ameibein	change	it has an indefinite shape
Blepharisma	blapharon	eyelid	it's shaped like a closed eyelid
Chlamydomonas	chlamyd- and chlamys	base and mantle	it looks like it's wearing a cloak
Coleps	koleos and ptilon	sheath and feather	probably because of the cilia surrounding its body
Colpidium	kolpos	fold or womb	it seems to have folds in its cell wall
Cyclops	kyklos and ops	round eye	is one-eyed
Daphnia	daphne	laurel or bay tree	it's shaped like a leaf of the laurel tree
Euglena	euglene	pupil of the eye	it has a reddish eyespot
Paramecium	paramekes	long oval	it has an oval shape
Rotifer	rota-	wheel	it has definite rings that rotate when vibrated
Stentor	stenein	very loud	it resembles a megaphone
Stylonychia	stylo-	pointed	its cilia appear pointed
Synura	syn- and ura	same tail	it has two tails
Volvox	volvere	to roll	it rolls around in the water
Vorticella	vortex and vertex	whirlpool and turning point	its top is whirlpool- shaped

---

FIELD ACTIVITY

2 STUDENT WORKSHEET

DISCOVERY LAB

Ditch's Brew

Double double, toil and trouble
Compost helps diminish the rubble!

Veggie scraps, some grass, and leaves
Give nitrogen that feeds our needs.
Wood chips, dry leaves, lint, and dust
Provide the carbon—that's a must!

Herbicides, plastic, ashes and meat—
don't use them for they're no treat.
Weeds, logs, and plants diseased
Are not what compost heaps will need.

Too much carbon won't break down,
Too much nitrogen stinks up the town
Equal parts of both, you see
Make the perfect recipe.

Compost adds organic stuff
So the soil has just enough.
Put your garden on a diet
Of healthy compost—won't you try it?

Double double, toil and trouble
Compost heaps eat up your rubble!

Objective

Compost a variety of materials to learn how different micro-organisms work together to break down organic matter.

Compost Contents 101

Decomposing organisms use the carbon and nitrogen in plants as nutrients. With the proper nutrients, the organisms will survive in a compost pile. You will collect materials to add to a compost pile. Find out what materials to collect by rereading the introduction and answering the questions below.

1. Which items can go into the compost pile?

Vegetable scraps, grass, leaves, wood chips, dry leaves, lint, and dust

can go into the compost pile.

2. Which items cannot go into the compost pile?

Herbicides, ashes, plastic, meat, logs, weeds, and diseased plants can-

not go into the compost pile.

3. What is the perfect recipe for a compost pile?

Equal parts of carbon-rich and nitrogen-rich matter make up the

perfect recipe for a compost pile.

MATERIALS

- 8–10 resealable plastic bags
- shovel
- water hose connected to a spigot (one per class)
- heat-resistant gloves (one per class)
- compost thermometer (one per class)

ANSWER KEY

ECOLABS & FIELD ACTIVITIES 101

Name _____ Date _____ Class _____

Recycle! Make Your Own Paper, continued

9. Separate the fibers of several cotton balls, and add them to the slurry to strengthen the paper. Stir the fibers into the slurry with a spoon until they are evenly distributed.

10. Use tape to label a towel with your name. Place the un-folded towel beside the pan. Hold the papermaker tape-side up. Scoop the papermaker into the slurry, and let it rest for a few minutes on the bottom of the pan. Fibers will settle on top of the papermaker.

11. Without tilting the papermaker, slowly lift it out of the pan. Let the water drain into the pan.

12. When the papermaker stops dripping, carefully flip it onto the towel so that the new paper lies between the paper-maker and the towel.

13. Gently press on the nylon with the sponge, and rub the sponge along the back of the mesh to absorb the water. Remove the excess water to strengthen your paper and to help it dry quickly. When your sponge is full of water, wring the water into the pan.

14. Repeat step 13 until you can no longer remove water from the paper.

15. Carefully lift the papermaker off of your new paper sheet. Gently lift the towel with the paper on it, and move it to the drying area. Congratulations! You have made your own paper!

16. Repeat steps 10–15 for each group member.

17. Discard any unused pulp mixture into a compost pile or a container that your teacher has provided. **Do not pour the slurry down the drain. Slurry clogs pipes.**

Analyzing Your Papermaking Process

18. Paper is made of dried plant fibers. What happened to the fibers in each of the steps you followed?

The Fate of the Fibers

Action	What happened to the fibers?
Step 1: Added water and blended the scrap paper	The fibers absorbed water and became mushy. The blender cut the fibers, making them shorter.
Step 2: Lifted the papermaker from the pan	The fibers were caught on the mesh of the nylon.
Step 3: Dried the paper	The meshed fibers contracted and became stuck together.

16 HOLT SCIENCE AND TECHNOLOGY

Name _____ Date _____ Class _____

The Case of the Ravenous Radish, continued

8. Mist your seeds every day using a spray bottle filled with water.

Collect Data

9. After your radishes have grown for about 20 days, make a table in your ScienceLog like the one below.

Radish Growth Observations

Crowded radishes	Width	Other observations	Uncrowded radishes	Width	Other observations
1	2 mm		1	20 mm	
2	4 mm		2	40 mm	

10. Gently remove the radishes from each hole on the "un-crowded" side of the box. With a metric ruler, measure the width of each radish, and record the width along with other observations in your ScienceLog.

11. Repeat step 11 for the "crowded" side of the box.

Analyze the Results

12. Was your prediction correct? Explain.

Sample answer: Yes, the radishes in the crowded environment were

much smaller.

13. What factor(s) appear to have affected the radishes' growth rates the most?

All radishes had equal amounts of water and light, so the amount of

nutrients available must have varied.

Draw Conclusions

14. How could space affect the supply of nutrients to a plant?

There is a fixed amount of nutrients available in the soil. Plants that

have to share the soil also have to share nutrients.

ECOLABS & FIELD ACTIVITIES **13**

Name _____ Date _____ Class _____

Survival Is Just a Roll of the Dice, continued

Analyze the Results

8. Did any team's pack die in either of the games? How?

Sample answer: Yes; my pack size was cut in half by disease in

Game 1. After that, too many pups died.

Critical Thinking

9. Considering what you learned in the game, could wolves overpopulate without human interference? Explain.

Sample answer: No; wolves face many constraints even when hu-

man interference is not a factor.

10. How could the disappearance of wolves from their ecosystem affect the populations of other species?

Sample answer: Species upon which wolves prey might might quickly

overpopulate and wipe out other parts of the food chain. Then

many more animal and plant species could be affected.

11. Do you feel this game accurately modeled the changing population of a wolf pack? Explain your answer.

Sample answer: Yes and no; there are so many factors that affect a

population that one would have to study a species in its environ-

ment to develop a more accurate model.

12. What could be done to improve the potential survival of your pack?

Sample answer: A habitat preserve could be set aside, and hunting

could be outlawed.

22   HOLT SCIENCE AND TECHNOLOGY

Name _____ Date _____ Class _____

Recycle! Make Your Own Paper, continued

19. How could this lab change to better conserve resources?

Sample answer: The lab could be changed by making less pulp and

using the leftovers from other groups.

20. How does recycling paper help the environment?

Sample answer: As more used resources are recycled, there is less

of a demand for new ones. Therefore, making recycled paper might

help conserve trees!

21. How can making paper from fibrous, nonwoody plants help the environment?

Sample answer: Less energy is used. Also, nonwoody plants grow

faster and can be replaced much more rapidly than trees.

Be an Artist!

22. Turn your paper into a work of art, such as a greeting card. Follow the steps below to add a little color to your paper. Your teacher will provide pigments made from fruits, vegetables, or spices.

23. Cut sponges into different shapes to form stamps.

24. Dip a stamp into a pigment. Press the stamp onto your sheet of paper. **Rinse your sponge before dipping it in another color.**

25. Dip the tip of a feather into the pigment, and use it as a pen to write a message or sign your masterpiece!

26. Let the pigment dry before handling your art.

DECORATING MATERIALS

- 3–4 sponges
- scissors
- bowl
- various natural pigments
- large feather
- water
- disposable gloves

HELPFUL HINT

Boiling the natural ingredients below left in water will make the corresponding pigment colors:

turmeric	orange
marigolds	yellow
onion peels	yellow
blueberries	blue
cranberries	red
raspberries	pink

▶▶ LIFE SCIENCE

ECOLABS & FIELD ACTIVITIES   17

Bacteria on Venus? continued

12. What could have caused the succession in your bottle?

Sample answer: As the microbes used the nutrients available, they also changed the types of nutrients, so other microbes thrived.

Draw Conclusions

13. Could sulfur-eating bacteria live in the atmosphere of Venus? Explain your answer.

Accept any well-reasoned answer. Sample answer (yes): Because sulfur, carbon, and traces of water vapor are in the clouds and in the atmosphere, sulfur-eating bacteria might live there. Airborne bacteria exist on Earth. Sample answer (no): If sulfur-eating bacteria live on Venus, scientists would have found it by now. Besides, the bacteria couldn't stay up in the clouds. They would fall to the surface.

Answers to Going Further
Students should read articles such as the following to learn about the use of bacteria to break down tires for reuse: Frazer, Lance. "Bacteria Breakfast," *Environmental Health Perspectives*, Vol. 104, No. 11, Nov. 1996. Or students can search for the articles on-line at the Environmental Health Information Services Web site.

Going Further

Believe it or not, the bacteria in your bottles can recycle old tires! Heat or chemical processing of rubber releases hazardous substances into the environment. But scientists have discovered that the types of bacteria you observed eat the sulfur in tires, breaking them down. The broken-down rubber can be made into new rubber tires that work as well as the original tires. The entire process is completely safe for the environment! Find out how used tires are disposed of in your community. Write a letter to a recycling plant or to a local landfill explaining the benefits of recycling tires with bacteria.

Bacteria on Venus? continued

SAFETY ALERT!
- Wear neoprene gloves and an apron. Do not touch your face or rub your skin, eyes, nose, or mouth.
- After the activity, clean your work area with disinfectant.
- Dispose of materials as instructed by your teacher, and wash your hands thoroughly.

HELPFUL HINT
Do not open the bottles during the experiment or your results may be negatively affected.

5. Shred the newspaper, a source of carbon, into small pieces, and add a handful to one pile of mud. To add sulfur, crush the egg shell, and crumble the white and yolk into the same pile of mud. Mix well.

6. Use the funnel to carefully add the plain mud to the bottle labeled "not enriched." Use the funnel to carefully add the nutrient-enriched mud to the bottle labeled "enriched."

7. Cap each bottle tightly. Place your bottles in an area where they will receive indirect sunlight.

8. Make a chart in your ScienceLog like the one below. Use colored pencils to sketch the contents of each bottle in your ScienceLog at least once a week for 6 weeks. Date each entry, compare the bottles, and comment on anything that surprises you.

Bottle Bacteria Data

Week	Date	Bottle with nutrients	Bottle without nutrients	Comments
1				
2				

Analyze the Results

9. When did each of the following types of microbes appear?

Green clumps: algae 3–15 days

Black spots: sulfate-reducing bacteria 6–21 days

Reddish purple spots: purple sulfur bacteria 2–3 weeks

Rust-colored areas: purple nonsulfur bacteria 1–3 weeks

10. In which bottle did the contents change more slowly?

Sample answer: The contents in the bottle without added nutrients changed more slowly.

11. What evidence of succession did you see?

Sample answer: The black spots disappeared as the purple spots appeared.

Name _____ Date _____ Class _____

Biome Adventure Travel, continued

4. Advertise your biome adventure with an original travel poster. Use illustrations and pictures to show features common to all of the destinations on your biome tour. Also include pictures of particular features for each place on the trip.

5. What characteristics are common to all of the destinations on your tour?
Sample answer: The tropical rain forest destinations share a temperature range of 20–30°C; annual precipitation of 200–400 cm; moist, thin topsoil; and broad-leaved evergreen trees and shrubs.

6. Although all of your destinations belong to the same biome, they differ in several ways. Describe the differences between your tour destinations.
Sample answer: Although each location supports life-forms characteristic to the tropical rain forest biome, each location has unique species. The humans, plants, and animals at each location have adapted differently to similar conditions.

7. Present your tour to another group. Use the poster and brochure to strengthen your sales pitch. Then pretend you are a tourist and listen as the other group tries to pitch their tour to you. Ask questions, and voice any concerns you may have. In your ScienceLog, list at least five things you learned from the other group's sales pitch about their biome.

Name _____ Date _____ Class _____

ECOLAB

7 STUDENT WORKSHEET

DISCOVERY LAB

Biome Adventure Travel

Earth Adventures Travel Agency

URGENT MEMO

To: All Staff
From: E. Cotore, Marketing Manager

Subject: Travel Package Concept

The hottest market in the travel biz is the ecotourism market. Ecotourists are travelers who visit natural areas while taking care not to damage the habitats they visit. To serve this market, we want to be the first to offer exciting tours to the world's major biomes.

Your assignment is to design and advertise a biome-adventure tour that takes travelers to at least four places around the globe. All of the tour destinations must belong to the same biome. For example, if you are designing a desert-biome tour, include visits to four or more deserts in different parts of the world. After you plan the tour, create an advertising campaign to promote the tour. Good luck!

MATERIALS
• world almanac and other geographical reference books
• travel magazines with photographs
• construction paper
• scissors
• butcher paper
• glue
• metric ruler
• colored markers
• map or globe

Objective
Learn about a particular biome by preparing a tour poster and a brochure.

Procedure
1. As a group, select a biome to research. Write the name of the biome below.
We will research the tropical rain forest **biome.**

2. Choose at least four tour destinations within that biome, and write them below.
Sample answer: Costa Rica, Trinidad, Indonesia, Malaysia

3. Research each destination. Use what you learn to create a tour brochure with an attractive design in order to persuade travelers to visit these destinations. Include practical information for the traveler, such as the following:
   • expected temperatures and rainfall in different seasons
   • native plants and animals
   • ecological, historical, and cultural points of interest
   • native foods
   • adaptations to the biome by the local people, and use of local materials in crafts

Name _____ Date _____ Class _____

DISCOVERY LAB

A Filter with Culture

The tiny town of Sweetwater is famous for its tasty, clean water and simple way of life. Tourists travel from hundreds of miles around just to sip the town's pure and refreshing water.

Last night a truck crashed, spilling a toxic chemical into Sweetwater's reservoir. Mayor H. Tuwo has declared a health emergency. Until the water is purified, residents will have no drinking water and farmers will have no water for their crops and animals. The tourists are leaving, and the residents may soon follow.

The town needs a fast and effective remedy. Mayor Tuwo has heard of your water-purification experiments with yeast. He has asked you to design a simple filtration system to remove the toxin from the town's water supply. Work quickly, or soon the town's name will be Dry Gulch!

SCIENTIFIC METHOD

Ask A Question

Which simple filter works most effectively to remove a sample pollutant from water?

Make a Prediction

1. You will investigate the effectiveness of three filters: charcoal, yeast, and yeast with charcoal. Which filter do you think will be most effective?

I think the _____ filter will be most effective.

Conduct an Experiment—Part 1: Test a Carbon Filter

2. **Day 1:** Trim seven coffee filters to fit inside the Büchner funnel. Place one filter inside the funnel.

3. Set the funnel over the beaker. Pack the carbon 1.25 cm high into the funnel. Place a second filter over the carbon.

4. Carefully pour in 250 mL of tap water to wet the activated carbon bed. After 5 minutes, discard the water that passed through the activated carbon bed.

5. Pour 100 mL of polluted water into an empty jar, screw on the lid, and label this jar "polluted water." Describe the polluted water.

The polluted water is purple.

6. Pour 100 mL of the polluted water into the activated carbon filter. Describe the water after it has passed through the carbon filter.

The water is less purple, but it is still very close to the color of the

original polluted water.

MATERIALS

- coffee filters
- scissors
- 40 mL polypropylene Büchner funnel
- 500 mL beaker
- 40 g of activated carbon granules
- metric ruler
- tap water
- protective gloves
- 500 mL of polluted water
- 4 glass jars with lids
- permanent marker
- baker's yeast

SAFETY ALERT!

Wear protective gloves when handling the polluted water. Do not drink any water from this activity.

Name _____ Date _____ Class _____

Biome Adventure Travel, continued

Analyze the Results

8. Would you like to tour the areas the other group advertised? Explain your answer.

Sample answer: Yes; visiting the tropical rain forest would provide

the opportunity to observe diverse plant and animal species not

found in the biome I live in.

9. How are biomes arranged around the globe? Explain your answer.

Generally speaking, due to the effect of solar intensity on climate,

tundra and taiga tend to be located near polar regions, deciduous

forests and grasslands occur at latitudes just below the tundra and

taiga, deserts mostly occur at latitudes near the Tropic of Cancer and

the Tropic of Capricorn, and tropical rain forests occur near the

equator.

10. Discuss any exceptions to this basic pattern.

Air circulation, ocean currents, the distribution of land masses, and

other factors all affect climate. As a result, conditions can exist that

allow different biomes to be interspersed among one another across

Earth.

Name _____ Date _____ Class _____

A Filter with Culture, continued

Analyze the Results

20. Compare the water samples in the three jars. Was your prediction correct? Explain your answer.

Sample answer: My prediction was correct. The combination filter

removed the color. The charcoal filter did not remove the purple

color. The yeast filter did not remove the cloudiness.

_____

21. List two advantages of using yeast and activated carbon to clean water.

Sample answer: Yeast and activated carbon are inexpensive and

effective.

_____

Draw Conclusions

22. Which filter would you recommend to the mayor of Sweetwater? Explain your answer.

I would recommend using the combined filter because it appeared

to remove all of the chemicals from the water.

_____

Critical Thinking

23. How could the town use this filtering method to process all the water in the reservoir?

Sample answer: A giant filter could be set up to process water

flowing out of the reservoir.

_____

HELPFUL HINT

After the activity, you may discard the yeast in a trash container.

Name _____ Date _____ Class _____

A Filter with Culture, continued

▶▶ **LIFE SCIENCE**

7. Pour some of the filtered water into a clean jar. Seal the jar, and label it "carbon-filtered water." Rinse the beaker.

8. Discard the filters and the charcoal. Rinse the funnel, and set it over the beaker.

Part 2: Test a Yeast Filter

9. Place a clean filter inside the funnel. Pour enough baker's yeast into the filter to form a layer 1.25 cm deep.

10. Carefully pour in 250 mL of tap water over the yeast to wet the yeast bed. After 5 minutes, discard the water that passed through the yeast bed.

11. Place a second filter on top of the yeast bed. Carefully pour 100 mL of polluted water into your yeast filter. Describe the water after it has passed through the filter.

The water is cloudy and has a light purple tint. Most of the purple

color is gone.

12. Day 2: Pour the filtered water into a clean, empty jar. Seal the jar, and label it "yeast-filtered water." Rinse the beaker.

13. Discard the filters and yeast. Rinse the funnel, and set it over the beaker.

Part 3: Test a Combination Filter

14. Place a clean filter inside the funnel. Pack activated carbon 1.25 cm deep in the funnel. Place a second filter on top of the activated carbon.

15. Pour approximately 250 mL (enough to wet the activated carbon layer) of tap water through the activated carbon filter.

16. Pour enough baker's yeast to form a layer 1.25 cm deep above the activated carbon filter.

17. Place the third filter on top of the yeast bed. Pour approximately 250 mL (enough to wet the yeast bed) of tap water through the yeast bed. After 5 minutes, discard the water that passed through the carbon and yeast beds.

18. Carefully pour 100 mL of polluted water into the yeast filter. Describe the water after it has passed through the filter.

The water is colorless.

19. Pour some of the filtered water into a clean, empty jar. Seal the jar, and label it "combination-filtered water."

Name _____ Date _____ Class _____

There's Something in the Air, continued

Analyze the Results

12. Which location had the highest measured level of ground ozone pollution?

Sample answer: The road sign near the busy intersection had the

highest amount of ground-level ozone pollution.

13. Compare your results with the results from other classes. During which part of the day was the ground-level ozone count the highest? Explain your answer.

Sample answer: The ozone count was highest between 1 P.M. and

4 P.M. Perhaps the afternoon heat caused more ozone formation.

Draw Conclusions

14. What atmospheric conditions seem to be connected with high levels of ozone pollution?

Sample answer: Areas with temperatures above 32°C, no wind, and

plenty of sunshine had higher levels of ozone pollution.

15. What can people do to reduce ozone levels on days when ground-level ozone might be high?

Sample answer: People can limit ozone-increasing activities, such as

driving, using gasoline-powered equipment, and using oil-based

paints, solvents, or varnishes. People can walk, bike, use public

transportation, or carpool.

Name _____ Date _____ Class _____

There's Something in the Air, continued

6. **Determine wind direction and cloud cover.** If the wind is too slight to move the string, wet your finger and hold it up. Face the direction that feels the coldest on your finger. Use the compass to determine which way you are facing. That is the direction of the wind. Record this direction and a cloud cover estimate in your ScienceLog.

7. **Retrieve the test strips.** After 1 hour of exposure, collect your indoor and outdoor test strips. At that time, record the temperatures at the test sites in your ScienceLog. Label the strips with the date, time, and location. Bring the test strips back to the classroom.

Collect Data

8. Compare the test strips to the colorimetric chart. Record your results in your ScienceLog in a table like the one below.

Pollution Data Table

	Temp	Wind direction	Wind speed (km/h)	Cloud cover (0-100%)	Eco Badge® reading (in ppb)	Safe/unsafe
Day 1 Indoor						
Outdoor						
Day 2 Indoor						
Outdoor						

9. The Environmental Protection Agency (EPA) has set the unsafe level for an hour of ground-level ozone exposure at 120 parts per billion (120 ppb). Indicate on the chart whether the ozone levels recorded were safe or unsafe.

10. Repeat steps 2–9 each day for 5 days.

Analyze the Results

11. How did wind, cloud cover, and temperature affect your ozone readings?

Sample answer: The ozone levels were higher on nonwindy, cloudy,

warm days than they were on windy, clear, cool days.

Name _____ Date _____ Class _____

Whether It Weathers (or Not), continued

21. Compare the percentages of mass lost for the rock types. Was the rate of chemical weathering faster on larger or smaller rocks?

The rate of chemical weathering is faster on smaller rocks than on

larger rocks of the same material.

22. How did the amount of exposed surface area affect the rate of weathering?

The rate of weathering depends on how much of the surface is ex-

posed.

23. Which design has more surface area, the statue or the obelisk? Explain your answer.

The statue has more surface area than the obelisk because it has

more small parts.

Draw Conclusions

24. Justify your choice of material and design.

Sample answer: I chose the obelisk because it does not have too

many small pieces that are going to weather quickly. The statue has

too much detail to withstand the forces of weathering in Rain Falls.

I would choose the granite obelisk because it would last the

longest.

Answer to Going Further:
To preserve the sculptures of Abraham Lincoln, Thomas Jefferson, George Washington, and Theodore Roosevelt, scientists have created a three-dimensional image of the internal fracture system. They have also developed computer-generated projections from a series of photographs of the sculpture to identify potentially unstable fractures. Some fractures have been injected with silicon to seal the cracks. Others will eventually be secured with steel pins to prevent further movement.

Going Further

Carved into the face of Mount Rushmore are giant sculptures of four American presidents. Find out how scientists are using new technology to preserve Mount Rushmore.

Name _____ Date _____ Class _____

Whether It Weathers (or Not), continued

HELPFUL HINT

Do not pour the samples down the drain when you are finished. Ask your teacher for the proper method of disposal.

16. Place a large piece of marble on a balance. Measure the initial mass, and record it in the table below. Place the marble in an empty beaker.

17. Repeat step 16 for the other materials, putting each rock into a different beaker.

18. Pour 50 mL of vinegar into each beaker. Observe and listen to the reaction. After 10 minutes, dispose of the vinegar as directed by your teacher.

19. Dry the rocks with a towel. Measure the final mass of each rock, and record the results in your ScienceLog. Calculate and record the percentage of rock lost, and record this value in the table below.

Analyze the Results

20. Overall, which rock best resisted weathering? Explain.

Granite had the best resistance to weathering because it did not

lose as much mass. Also it was not affected by the vinegar or the

freezing-and-thawing test.

Rock Weathering Results

Rock	Marble	Granite	Limestone	Concrete
Effect of freezing and thawing the rock	one tiny crack	no visible change	a few cracks	a lot of cracks
Initial mass of rock before shaking (g)	100 g	100 g	100 g	100 g
Final mass of rock after shaking (g)				
Percentage of mass lost				
Initial mass of small rocks before vinegar (g)				
Initial mass of small rocks after vinegar (g)				
Percentage of mass lost				
Initial mass of large rocks before vinegar (g)				
Initial mass of large rocks after vinegar (g)				
Percentage of mass lost				

Name _____ Date _____ Class _____

The Frogs Are Off Course, continued

8. Were any of the test results different from what you expected? If so, which were different and how might you explain these differences?

Sample answer: The dissolved oxygen level was higher in the water leaving the golf course. This may be because the stream becomes very rocky before it leaves the golf course, causing more air to be added to the water. The stream is deeper and slower upstream.

Draw Conclusions

9. Which explanation of the frogs' disappearance is supported by your tests? Explain your answer.

Sample answer: The elevated nutrient levels in the water leaving the golf course support the city's explanation.

Critical Thinking

10. How might a country club maintain a green turf while decreasing the amount of polluted runoff?

Sample answer: A country club could use less fertilizer, carefully choose what type of fertilizer to use, or choose grasses that are better adapted to local conditions.

11. Frogs are just one organism affected by the runoff. What other organisms could be affected?

Sample answer: Fish require dissolved oxygen in order to survive. The rapid growth of algae depletes the stream of dissolved oxygen; this depletion adversely affects fish.

Name _____ Date _____ Class _____

The Frogs Are Off Course, continued

4. **At the collection sites:** Where the stream enters the golf course, label and fill jar 4 with water. Where the stream exits the golf course, label and fill jar 5 with water.

5. **In class:** Conduct each of the five water-quality tests on each sample. Record the results in the table below.

Test Kit Results

Jar	Contents	Phosphate	Nitrite/nitrate	Ammonia	pH	Amount of dissolved oxygen
1	Distilled water					
2	Tap water					
3	Tap water with plant food					
4	Water entering					
5	Water exiting					

Analyze the Results

6. Were the nutrient levels of the water entering the golf course the same as those of the water leaving it?

Sample answer: No, the water leaving the golf course contained more nutrients than the water entering the golf course.

7. Were there traces of nutrients in the water entering the golf course? Explain your answer.

Sample answer: Yes, the stream naturally has nutrients from the plants and animals.

Operation Oil-Spill Cleanup, continued

11. What happened when the oil reached the beach? How effective was the cleanup of sand and wildlife?

Sample answer: Oil penetrated the sand and the fur, feathers, and skin of animals. Oil was extremely difficult to remove from the animals.

12. What factors might make a real cleanup different from your simulation?

Winds, currents, temperature, salinity of the water, and the type or weight of the oil would affect results, as would large-scale availability of cleanup materials.

Communicate Results

13. After all teams have finished their cleanup, present your results to the class. Vote to determine which plan should be submitted to Megacrude Oil Company.

14. Which cleanup plan worked best? Explain your answer.

Accept all reasonable answers.

Critical Thinking

15. In a real oil spill, how might cleanup methods affect animal life?

Sample answer: Cleanup methods using detergents or hot, pressurized water might harm animals.

Operation Oil-Spill Cleanup, continued

Evaluation of Cleaning Supplies

Cleaning material	Oil-spill containment	Water cleanup & oil recovery	Shore cleanup	Wildlife cleanup	Environmental impact

Draw Conclusions

5. As a team, decide which materials were most effective at cleaning up the oil. Determine which materials and techniques your team will use for each of the following:
- oil-spill containment
- water cleanup and oil recovery
- cleanup of shore and wildlife
- minimization of the impact of your cleanup operations on the ocean ecosystem

6. Devise a plan. Summarize the important components of each idea you came up with in step 5. Based on your discussion, develop a plan in your ScienceLog for how your team can best accomplish the cleanup. Write detailed instructions for cleaning up an oil spill with the supplies you tested.

7. Build a model. Build a model ocean in a pan. Create a shore using sand, gravel, and a few rocks at one end of the pan. Place a feather and a fur strip at the shoreline.

8. Carefully add 0.5 L of water. Let a small beaker of oil represent your supertanker. Spill 50 mL of oil into the center of your water area. Gently blow the oil toward the shore.

9. Test your plan. Check the time, and implement the cleanup plan as quickly as possible. For each cleanup task listed in step 5 (oil-spill containment, oil recovery, shore cleanup, and wildlife cleanup), record how long it takes to complete the task and how well the cleanup works in your ScienceLog.

Analyze Results

10. Was it possible to recover any of the oil? Could the recovery method that worked best be used in a real oil spill?

Sample answer: Oil could be recovered. This would be difficult but possible on a large scale.

HELPFUL HINT

Protect your clothing from oil by wearing an apron during the oil-spill cleanup.

That Greenhouse Effect! continued

Test the Hypothesis

10. Test your hypothesis. Create a data table in your ScienceLog similar to the one you made before. Describe the conditions of each jar listed in the column headings. Be sure to cover both jars with plastic wrap. Record the results of your experiment in the table. Graph your data. Note any changes you made to your experiment.

Analyze the Results

11. Was your prediction correct? Explain.

Sample answer: Yes, the air over the dry soil was warmer than the

air over the wet soil.

12. How did the experiment model the variation in warming in different parts of the world?

Sample answer: Arid regions should contribute more heat to the at-

mosphere than nonarid regions contribute.

13. How does your model differ from the real "greenhouse Earth?"

Sample answer: The experimental model does not account for the

interaction between arid and nonarid regions, nor does it take into

account human modification of the environment.

That Greenhouse Effect! continued

Sample answers:

Greenhouse-Model Temperature Data

Observation point	Temperature (°C) control jar	Temperature (°C) experimental jar
Initial temperature in the sun	23°C	23°C
2 min	25.5°C	28.5°C
4 min	25.5°C	33°C
6 min	26°C	35°C
8 min	26°C	37°C
10 min	28°C	40°C

Form a Hypothesis: Round 2

7. Many scientists believe that the Earth's surface will heat up as greenhouse gases build up in the atmosphere. But they don't expect all parts of the Earth to warm equally. Consider the following questions:
   - Which will heat faster, the air over snow-covered plains or the air over newly plowed fields?
   - Which will heat faster, air over the ocean or air over land?
   - Does vegetation affect the rate of global warming?
   - How does the amount of moisture in the soil affect the rate of global warming?
   - Does the temperature of the land affect the temperature of the air above it?

   Generate a hypothesis based on one of the questions, and record the hypothesis in your ScienceLog.

Make a Prediction

8. Design an experiment that will test your hypothesis. Reuse the jars you used in steps 1–6. Sketch your design in your ScienceLog.

9. Based on your experimental design in step 8, predict the results that you expect. Write your prediction below.

   Sample prediction: In two covered jars placed in sunlight, the

   temperature of the air over the dry soil will increase faster than the

   temperature of the air over the wet soil.

Name _____ Date _____ Class _____

What's All the Flap About? continued

Putting It All Together

7. How do birds produce thrust?

Birds flap their wings to push themselves forward through air.

8. How did your airplane produce thrust?

I pushed the plane to give it thrust.

9. How does the shape of the wings help a bird fly?

A bird's wings are thin, so the wing can glide easily through the air with little drag. The wings' width helps create lift and thrust during flapping by pushing air downward and backward.

10. How do birds overcome their weight to produce lift?

Birds' bodies are lightweight and streamlined. As birds flap their wings to produce thrust, the speed of the air flowing over their wings increases. Faster-flowing air causes lift. When lift is greater than the bird's weight, the bird rises in the air.

11. After observing birds in flight and constructing a simple flying machine, what can you report back to DaVinci about the possibilities of human flight?

Sample answer: Human flight is possible if there is enough thrust to overcome the weight of the cargo, producing lift.

Answer to Going Further: When a bird flaps its wings, a rush of air creates circular air movement behind both sides of the wings. Birds often fly in a V formation to take advantage of this effect. By flying slightly to the side of and behind another bird, a bird can catch the air moving upward from the wings of the bird in the lead. This gives the bird a lift, and the bird expends less energy to fly.

Going Further

Find out why traveling in a V formation enables a flock of birds to use less energy in flight. In fact, birds flying in this formation use half the energy they would use if they were each flying solo!

▶▶ EARTH SCIENCE ◀◀

Name _____ Date _____ Class _____

Rain Maker or Rain Faker? continued

12. Measure the **temperature** using the dry-bulb thermometer. Record your data in your ScienceLog.

13. Measure the **atmospheric pressure** using the barometer. Record your data in your ScienceLog.

14. Measure the **wind speed** using the anemometer, if available. Record your data in your ScienceLog.

15. Measure the **rainfall** using the rain gauge. Without disturbing the jar, read the mark that is aligned with the water level. Record your data in your ScienceLog.

Make a Prediction—Measurement-Based

16. Predict the weather based on your measurements in the second prediction row of your chart.

Analyze the Results

You made predictions using different types of information. One type was based on weather proverbs and observations, and the other type was based on measurements from instruments. Answer the questions below in your ScienceLog.

17. At home: Observe the weather when you're not at school, and record your observations. Compare your two predictions. Was either prediction correct? Was one more reliable than the other?

Sample answer: One morning I predicted that it would rain, and it

did. In class, our pressure measurement suggested that the sky

should clear, and it did.

18. Did the proverbs help you to predict the weather? Give an example.

Sample answer: Yes, the cloud and the dew proverbs seemed to

hold true, although the clouds didn't always bring the expected rain.

Draw Conclusions

19. Write a one-page paper persuading farmers to predict weather on their own. How would you tell the farmers of Nigh Eve to forecast the weather using only observations (no instruments). Explain which instruments they might find most useful in making accurate predictions.

Name _____ Date _____ Class _____

Energy-Efficient Home, continued

Ask a Question

14. How can you improve your home's performance?

Sample answer: The home's performance can be improved by

covering the windows and by making them smaller.

_____

Form a Hypothesis

15. With your group, design an energy-efficient home design that best improves your model's insulating ability. Consider the following design features:
- location and surface area of windows
- roof overhang
- type of insulation
- interior and exterior surface colors and finishes
- air leakage around windows, doors, etc.

16. Based on your discussion, record a hypothesis in your ScienceLog about what kind of energy-efficient home will best save energy resources. Sketch your experimental model design in your ScienceLog.

Test the Hypothesis

17. After your teacher has approved your design, modify the box to build your new, improved model.

18. Repeat steps 12–13 to test your design, and record your results in the table on page 81.

Analyze the Results

In your ScienceLog, answer the following questions:

19. How do you account for any difference in the effectiveness of your two models?

20. Compare your results with the results of other groups. Were their designs more efficient? If so, what did they do differently? If you could redesign your model, what changes would you make?

Name _____ Date _____ Class _____

Energy-Efficient Home, continued

9. Which is a more effective insulator, tightly packed material or loosely packed material? Explain your answer.

Sample answer: Loosely packed insulation is more effective than

tightly packed insulation because it contains more air spaces.

Draw Conclusions

10. Which material would you choose to insulate a house?

Sample answer: I would choose either cellulose, rock wool, or

plastic foam.

_____

Part 2: Model an Energy-Efficient Home

Now that you have a good idea of what materials make good insulators, build a model of an energy-efficient home. Then make a second model home, adding features to improve its insulating efficiency.

MATERIALS
- scissors
- cardboard box with lid
- metric ruler
- clear plastic wrap
- transparent tape
- thermometer
- one or more of the following: caulk, paint, colored construction paper

11. Cut a 5 × 5 cm window in a cardboard box. Cover the window with plastic wrap, and tape it in place. Place a thermometer in the model so that it can be seen through the window. Tape the thermometer in place.

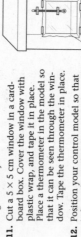

12. Position your control model so that it faces the sun to allow the most sunlight to enter the window.

13. Record the temperature in the model at the start of this experiment and every 5 minutes for 30 minutes.

PHYSICAL SCIENCE

Model Home Temperatures

	Start	5 min	10 min	15 min	20 min	25 min	30 min
Control temperature (°C)							
Experimental temperature (°C)							

Name _____ Date _____ Class _____

Greener Cleaners, continued

10. How did the acids, bases, or abrasives in eco-friendly cleaners compare in strength with the ingredients often contained in commercial products? Explain.

The ingredients in eco-friendly cleaners are much weaker acids,

bases, or abrasives than those in commercial products.

_____

11. Would you use eco-friendly cleaners instead of commercial cleaners? Explain your answer.

Sample answer: Yes; ecofriendly cleaners can be used to avoid

health hazards, to avoid storage and disposal difficulties, or to re-

duce the risk to the environment. Eco-friendly cleaners cost less.

_____

12. Are eco-friendly cleaners always safe?

No, the natural acids and bases in them could be hazardous if not

used properly.

_____

Critical Thinking

13. Many household cleaners are sold in unnecessary or nonrecyclable packaging. How could you cut down on excess packaging?

Sample answer: I can buy cleaners in bulk to save money and to cut

down on unnecessary trips to the store. I could also buy cleaners in

recyclable packages, such as cardboard boxes or recyclable plastic

bottles.

Name _____ Date _____ Class _____

Greener Cleaners, continued

SAFETY ALERT!

• Wear an apron, goggles, and protective gloves. Spilled liquid on floors is hazardous.
• Be sure to read and follow safety warnings on all products. Do not touch your eyes, nose, mouth, or face. Wash your hands thoroughly after handling cleansers.

2. Use the eco-friendly product on a portion of the test area until the product has done its job as well as possible.

3. Use the commercial product on another portion of the test area until the product has done its job as well as possible.

4. Repeat steps 1–3 until you have been to all four stations. In your ScienceLog, note the effectiveness of the product at each station.

You Be the Judge

5. Which of the eco-friendly ingredients have acidic properties? (Hint: You can find out by touching pH paper to the cleaner.)

The vinegar and lemon juice have acidic properties.

6. Which of the eco-friendly ingredients have properties of bases? (Hint: You can find out by touching pH paper to the cleaner.)

The baking soda has a basic property.

7. Which of the eco-friendly ingredients have absorbent properties?

The chalk has absorbent properties.

8. Which of the eco-friendly ingredients have abrasive properties?

The paste made of baking soda has abrasive properties.

9. How do you think these cleaners work?

Acids and bases bond with the molecules in the stain and break the

chemical bonds between the stain and the surface. Cleaners with ab-

sorbent and abrasive properties physically break the bonds between

the stain and the surface.

Name _____ Date _____ Class _____

A Light Current of Air, continued

21. In this activity, the wind that drives the windmills is probably not a renewable source of energy. Why is this true?

Sample answer: Electricity powers the wind source (the blow dryer), which probably comes from a nonrenewable energy source.

22. For what other purposes could you use the rotation of a turbine?

Sample answer: The windmill could lift heavy objects, grind flour, or power a water pump.

23. List other ways to move the turbine.

Sample answer: The windmill could be turned by water from a dam or river or by steam. You could also manually turn the turbine with a crank.

24. If the wind isn't blowing, and you have a choice of burning coal or biomass to generate electricity, which would you choose? Explain.

Sample answer: I would choose biomass because it is a renewable energy source.

Going Further

Have you ever seen someone push-start a car after the battery has been discharged? Explain in your ScienceLog how pushing the car helps start it.

Answer to Going Further: As the car moves, it manually rotates a magnet close to a coiled wire. When the car is put in gear, a connection allows the charge to travel to the spark plugs, which then start the car.

Name _____ Date _____ Class _____

A Light Current of Air, continued

Correct

Incorrect

13. If the magnet or pencil wobbles as it spins, adjust it so that one end of the pencil points to the center of the magnet. Also adjust the pipe cleaners around the pencil; just a slight movement can change how much the magnet wobbles. Be patient; the alignment must be exact for the windmill to produce electricity.

14. Once the voltmeter consistently shows over 1 V, disconnect the voltmeter, and clip the alligator clips and wire assembly to each wire of an LED.

15. Repeat steps 11–13 so that the LED glows. Wow! You've just run a small light using a wind-powered generator.

16. Repeat steps 11–13 so that the LED glows again. Now, rotate the coil so that the rotating magnet points in the same direction as the coil.

Analyze the Results

17. What happened when you rotated the coil? Why?

The LED stopped glowing. The coil must be at right angles to the magnet to generate electricity.

18. Why would you want to use wind energy instead of other forms of energy? Explain your answer.

Sample answer: Many of Earth's energy resources are limited, so it is necessary to develop and use renewable sources of energy. Wind is a renewable energy source.

19. What are some of the disadvantages of using wind energy?

Sample answer: The wind might not be blowing fast enough or in the right direction to be able to use it.

20. How might you solve these problems?

Sample answer: Pivoting turbines could adjust for the wind's direction. You might need to build several windmills.

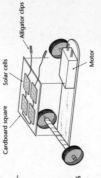

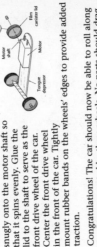

Name _____ Date _____ Class _____

Photon Drive, continued

6. Cut a tiny hole in the middle of the third lid. Push the lid snugly onto the motor shaft so that it spins evenly. Glue the lid to the shaft to serve as the front drive wheel of the car. Center the front drive wheel in the front of the car. Tightly mount rubber bands on the wheels' edges to provide added traction.

7. Congratulations! The car should now be able to roll along the floor supported by three wheels. No parts should drag.

8. Use hook-and-loop adhesive tape to mount the four solar cells side-by-side on the cardboard square, as shown. Then connect the solar cells with wires, as shown.

9. Use rubber bands to mount the solar cell unit on top of the tongue depressor. Use alligator clips to connect the free ends of the wires to the posts of the motor, as shown below.

10. Add enough modeling clay to the cardboard on the side opposite the motor to ensure that the car runs in a straight line.

Analysis

11. How could you modify your solar car to make it faster?

Sample answer: I could use more solar cells, add reflectors, or angle

the cells to collect more light.

12. Modify your car so that it goes faster. Place your car on the starting line. At your teacher's mark, start your car and let it travel to the finish line.

Name _____ Date _____ Class _____

An Earful of Sounds, continued

Sound Off!

10. Look over your list of responses on page 94 and think about what certain sounds might have in common. Is there a pattern to the types of sounds you found irritating or calming? Explain your answer.

Sample answer: Most really loud, high-pitched, sharp sounds are irri-

tating, while soft, lower sounds are usually calming.

11. What is your definition of noise pollution?

Sample answer: Sharp, sudden sounds are irritating and contribute

to noise pollution.

12. Based on your observations, what types of sounds do you feel contribute most to noise pollution?

Sample answer: Honking horns and moving trucks cause a lot of

irritating noise.

Critical Thinking

13. What could be done in your community to reduce noise pollution?

Sample answer: Trees could be planted between my home and the

street. The trees would act as a sound barrier and at the same time

they would attract birds, which produce more pleasing sounds.

Name _____ Date _____ Class _____

Photon Drive, continued

13. Compare the performance of your car with that of the other cars in the class. Whose car went the fastest and the straightest? How did the designs of your classmates differ from yours?

Sample answer: Unlike my car, the fastest car had reflectors that

directed sunlight onto the solar cells. The straightest car had clay

near the front of the car.

Critical Thinking

14. When automobiles burn gasoline, the combustion process leads to the creation of small amounts of ozone, a highly reactive form of oxygen, which is a main component of smog. What advantages does a solar car have over a gasoline-powered automobile?

Solar cars do not burn fuel, so they do not release hydrocarbons like

a gas-powered automobile does. Therefore, solar cars do not con-

tribute to ground-level ozone.

15. What problems prevent us from making all cars solar?

Sample answer: Not all areas in the world have lots of sun. Some

areas of the world stay very cloudy, which would affect a solar car's

performance. Also, there is a limited amount of energy that can be

extracted from a given amount of sunlit surface.

16. How could these problems be solved?

Sample answer: If sunlight could be stored for later use, the car

would run regardless of the weather.